Empowering
Self-Esteem for Young Boys
Building Confidence and
Strength

Empowering
Self-Esteem for Young Boys
Building Confidence and Strength

11 Inspiring Stories That Foster Self-Confidence for Teens and Encourage Growth Mindset

Aria Capri Publishing Group
Devon Abbruzzese
Mauricio Vasquez

Toronto, Canada

Authors:
Aria Capri Publishing Group
Devon Abbruzzese
Mauricio Vasquez

First Printing: February 2025

ISBN 978-1-998729-06-7 (Paperback)
ISBN 978-1-998729-07-4 (Hardcover)
ISBN 978-1-998729-08-1 (Ebook)

To our son, Leonardo

You are the heart and inspiration behind every page of this book. Your courage, curiosity, and strength remind us daily why believing in ourselves is the greatest gift we can give.

Unlock More Inspiration for Your Teen!

Loved this book? There's more waiting for your son (and/or daughter)! Scan the QR code to explore:

- Uplifting stories and tools for building confidence.
- Workbooks to boost self-esteem and resilience.
- Exclusive tips for thriving in today's world.

💜 **Scan Now and keep the journey going!**

Join Our Exclusive Community

Ready to continue your journey beyond these pages? We'd love to connect. By joining our exclusive community, you'll:

- Get First Dibs on New Releases: Be the first to know about upcoming books and special projects.
- Access Exclusive Content & Perks: Enjoy behind-the-scenes insights, bonus resources, and priority invitations.
- Shape Future Works: Your feedback directly influences what we create next, making you part of the process.

Sound exciting? Scan the QR code. We can't wait to welcome you and share even more inspiration, guidance, and opportunities to grow—together!

Thanks for joining our exclusive circle, brought to you by Aria Capri Publishing, a company of MindScape Artwork!

Join Aria Capri Publishing on Patreon

Love the content so far? Stay even more connected with exclusive behind-the-scenes insights, patron-only perks, and sneak peeks of upcoming projects.

Simply scan this QR code (or follow the link) to become a patron and unlock a deeper level of engagement and support!

https://patreon.com/AriaCapriPublishing

Table of Contents

Introduction

Welcome to a collection of stories about courage, growth, and self-discovery. In these pages, you'll meet eleven young boys, each navigating the challenges that come with figuring out who they are and where they belong. From academic pressure to fitting in, these characters face struggles that might feel familiar. But beyond the challenges, these stories offer something more: a journey toward building self-confidence and self-esteem.

Being a teenager can be tough. There's pressure to excel in school, keep up with trends, meet expectations, and fit into an ever-changing world. It's easy to feel like you're not enough or that you need to be perfect to be valued. But perfection is a myth, and your worth isn't tied to how you measure up against impossible standards. This book is here to remind you of that truth.

Each story in this collection explores a different challenge, but at their core, they all share the same message: confidence doesn't come from being flawless, and self-esteem isn't about seeking approval from others. Instead, it's about embracing your unique qualities, learning from your experiences, and realizing that you are worthy just as you are.

Through their journeys, the characters in this book discover that true confidence comes from within. They learn to navigate setbacks, face their fears, and celebrate their individuality. Whether it's finding strength after a stumble, embracing their creative passions, or learning to speak up, each character takes steps toward becoming their most authentic selves.

This book is for anyone who's ever felt unsure of themselves, who's doubted their abilities, or who's struggled to feel like they belong. It's for those who want to feel more confident in their own skin and believe in their worth.

As you read these stories, I hope you'll see reflections of your own experiences. I hope you'll feel inspired by these characters' resilience and reminded that confidence and self-esteem are built, not handed out. It's okay to make mistakes. It's okay to feel vulnerable. And it's more than okay to be exactly who you are.

So, let's begin. Together, let's explore the powerful, messy, and beautiful process of becoming your best, most confident self. The journey starts here.

Share the Wisdom

Dear Valued Reader,

Thank you for choosing this book to inspire confidence and growth in the teen boys in your life. Your feedback means so much to me and helps others discover these empowering stories.

As an independent author, your review plays a vital role in spreading this book's message. Simply scan the QR code below to share your thoughts—it only takes a moment but makes a big difference.

Your support means the world, and we are truly grateful.

With gratitude,

Devon & Mauricio

How to Use This Book

Welcome! You're holding a book that's more than just a collection of stories. It's a journey, a guide, and, hopefully, a friend that will help you navigate some of life's most challenging moments. Whether you're here to find inspiration, gain confidence, or simply connect with characters who feel as real as your own reflections, this book is designed to meet you where you are.

Start Where You Need

Each chapter in this book introduces a different character, facing challenges that might feel familiar to you. From dealing with perfectionism to struggling with self-expression, every story touches on themes of resilience, self-confidence, and self-esteem. You don't need to read the stories in order; think of this book as a toolbox. Start with the story that speaks to you most, whether it's about overcoming fear of failure, embracing your individuality, or finding balance in your life.

Reflect and Relate

After each story, take a moment to reflect. Ask yourself:

- What parts of this story resonate with me?
- Have I faced similar challenges? How did I respond?
- What can I learn from the character's journey?

You'll notice that the characters often have internal monologues that reflect their thoughts and emotions. Use these moments to connect with your own feelings. You might even want to jot down your thoughts in a journal. Consider writing about your own experiences, victories, or even the things that still feel like struggles. There's power in putting your thoughts into words.

Take Small Steps

The lessons in this book aren't about making grand changes overnight. Instead, they're about recognizing small, meaningful shifts. Perhaps one story inspires you to speak up a little more in class. Another might encourage you to take a break when you're feeling overwhelmed. Each step, no matter how small, brings you closer to embracing your unique strengths and growing your confidence.

Use the Pause Moments

Throughout the book, you'll find moments where the characters pause to reflect, often through an internal thought or a conversation with a mentor. These are your prompts to pause, too. Think about what advice you would give to a friend in a similar situation—or what advice you'd like to hear for yourself. This book is as much about learning from others as it is about learning from within.

Share and Discuss

Sometimes, the best way to understand something is by sharing it. If a particular story moves you, talk about it with a friend, parent, or teacher. Sharing your thoughts can spark meaningful conversations and help you see that you're not alone in your experiences.

Be Kind to Yourself

This book is about embracing who you are, imperfections and all. As you read, remember: growth isn't linear, and it's okay to have setbacks. The characters in these stories don't achieve their breakthroughs in a single moment—they stumble, they reflect, and they rise again. Allow yourself the same grace.

A Journey for Today—and Tomorrow

You might find yourself coming back to this book at different points in your life. What resonates today might feel different a few months or years from now. That's the beauty of growth—it's ongoing. Let this book be a companion on your journey, reminding you that every challenge is an opportunity to learn, and every setback is a chance to rise.

Final Thoughts

You are capable of incredible things. This book is here to remind you of that. Each story is a mirror, reflecting the strength, courage, and resilience that already exist within you. Take your time, be patient with yourself, and remember: your worth isn't defined by achievements or external validation. It's found in the way you embrace your true self, every single day.

Now, let's begin. Your journey awaits.

Story 1 - Finding His Courage

Eli stood in front of his bedroom door, his soccer jersey clutched tightly in his hands. His reflection in the doorknob stared back at him, distorted but all too familiar. He wasn't sure why, but that small, warped image always felt like the clearest version of himself—imperfect, out of place, and trying too hard.

No matter how much he practiced, Eli couldn't shake the feeling that he wasn't good enough. He'd spent hours in the backyard with the soccer ball, imagining the roar of a crowd, but all he ever seemed to hear was the sharp voice of doubt in his head. *"Why can't I be as fast as Daniel or as good as Noah?"* he thought, his chest tightening. He brushed a hand through his messy hair, giving up when it wouldn't lie flat.

At school, the weight of inadequacy seemed to press harder with each step he took down the hallway. Eli walked with his head down, avoiding eye contact with his classmates. His ears burned as he overheard a group of boys laughing at the end of the hall. He wasn't sure what they were laughing about, but it was easy to imagine they were laughing at him.

"Eli, you're such a klutz," someone had joked during P.E. last week when he'd tripped over his own feet during a practice scrimmage. Eli hadn't laughed. Moments like that stuck with him, replaying in his mind whenever he tried to be brave.

The day crawled by in a haze of worksheets, lectures, and the dull ache of self-doubt. By the time the final bell rang, Eli was already planning his escape route to avoid being noticed. But his plan was derailed as the principal's voice echoed over the loudspeaker, announcing a school-wide skills competition. The cafeteria buzzed with excitement. For a moment, Eli's heart skipped.

The competition wasn't just about soccer—it would include different activities: music, art, sports, even solving puzzles. It was a chance for anyone to showcase their unique talents. Eli's mind immediately went to soccer. It was the one thing he loved more than anything, even if he wasn't sure he was good enough to compete.

"You'd have to be one of the best to even try," said a voice from across the room. Eli glanced over and saw Daniel leaning casually against the wall, surrounded by a group of boys. Daniel's confidence seemed to fill the room, and Eli felt himself shrinking.

Daniel was right, wasn't he? Eli had no business signing up for something like this. His stomach churned at the thought of being watched, judged, and laughed at. He slung his backpack over his shoulder and left the cafeteria quickly, pushing the idea out of his mind.

After school, Eli found himself kicking a soccer ball alone behind the bleachers. The quiet field was his favorite place, a space where he could forget about being compared to others. As he practiced, lost in thought, he didn't notice Coach Miller approaching from the sidelines.

"*Nice footwork, Eli,*" Coach Miller said, his voice calm but steady.

Eli froze, the ball rolling to a stop. "*Oh, um, thanks,*" he muttered, his face turning red.

"*I've seen you out here practicing after school,*" Coach continued. "*You've got talent, kid. Why didn't I see your name on the sign-up sheet for the competition?*"

Eli shifted uncomfortably, his gaze fixed on the ground. "*I don't think I'm good enough,*" he admitted. "*I'm not like Daniel or the other guys. I'd just embarrass myself.*"

"*Eli, talent isn't about being the best,*" Coach said firmly. "*It's about doing what you love and giving it your all. Do you love playing soccer?*"

Eli hesitated, then nodded. "*Yeah, I do.*"

"*Then don't let fear stop you,*" Coach said, clapping Eli on the shoulder. "*I've seen you work hard out here when no one's watching. That kind of effort matters more than being flashy. The only thing holding you back is the belief that you don't belong out there.*"

As Coach walked away, his words echoed in Eli's mind. Maybe—just maybe—he could take the first step. But the doubts still lingered, tugging at him like a heavy chain.

That afternoon, Eli stood in front of the sign-up sheet in the empty hallway. His hand hovered over the pen, his chest tightening with indecision. The doubts swirled around him, whispering that he'd never be as good as the others.

But then he thought about what Coach Miller had said: "*The only thing holding you back is the belief that you don't belong.*"

Taking a deep breath, Eli forced his hand to steady and quickly scribbled his name on the sign-up sheet. The letters weren't neat, and they leaned awkwardly to the side, but they were there—his first step toward something new, something terrifying. The weight of the pen felt heavier than he'd expected, as though writing his name wasn't just about entering a competition but about making a promise to himself.

As soon as he stepped back, a wave of anxiety hit him. "*What have I done?*" Eli thought, his heart hammering in his chest. He could almost hear Daniel and the others teasing him. "*What if I mess up? What if they laugh?*" The fear gripped him like a vise. But underneath that fear, there was something else—a small spark, a flicker of pride. For once, he hadn't let the fear take control.

The days leading up to the competition were a blur of practice and nerves. Every afternoon, Eli found himself on the empty soccer field, trying to perfect his penalty kicks. But it wasn't just his feet that felt shaky—his whole body felt heavy with doubt.

"*Relax, Eli,*" Coach Miller said one afternoon, watching from the sidelines. "*You're overthinking. Just focus on why you love the game.*"

Eli nodded, but it wasn't that simple. Every time he lined up for a shot, he could feel the imaginary stares of an audience, hear their whispers of criticism. The first few kicks were weak and off-target. Eli winced as the ball skidded past the goal.

"*Try again,*" Coach said, his tone steady but encouraging. "*Close your eyes if you need to, but remember why you're here.*"

Taking a deep breath, Eli closed his eyes. The pressure of the competition, the fear of judgment—it all faded as he focused on the feel of the ball beneath his foot, the rhythm of his steps, and the sound of his own heartbeat. With a final exhale, he kicked. The ball soared cleanly into the top corner of the goal.

When Eli opened his eyes, Coach was smiling. "*That's what I'm talking about,*" he said. "*You've got this, Eli. You're stronger than you think.*"

For a moment, Eli felt lighter, almost confident. But as the competition drew closer, the doubts crept back in like shadows.

The night before the big day, Eli sat on his bed, the soccer ball resting on his lap. He turned it slowly in his hands, tracing the black and white panels with his fingers. His thoughts raced: *"What if I trip? What if I miss every shot? What if they think I don't belong there?"*

"You're unique, Eli. And that's your strength." Coach Miller's words echoed in his mind, a steadying anchor in the storm of self-doubt.

Eli closed his eyes and tried to imagine the moment. Instead of picturing the faces of his classmates or the judging eyes of Daniel and the others, he saw himself on the field—alone, just him and the ball. No expectations, no audience, just the joy of playing the game he loved.

A new thought began to take shape: *"What if this isn't about them? What if it's about proving to myself that I can do this?"*

The idea was both terrifying and freeing. Eli opened his eyes, gripping the ball with a newfound resolve. Tomorrow, he would step onto that field—not to prove something to Daniel or anyone else, but to prove something to himself.

The next morning arrived in a rush of nerves and anticipation. Eli could barely concentrate during class, his mind filled with images of the field and the competition. By the time the final bell rang, his stomach churned with a mix of fear and excitement.

When Eli stepped into the gym, the sound of other kids practicing and the hum of conversations filled the air. He clutched his soccer ball tightly, his palms damp with sweat. As he stood at the edge of the room, waiting for his turn, the voices around him faded into the background. He took a deep breath, replaying Coach Miller's words in his mind: *"Focus on why you love the game."*

Eli's heart pounded as his name was called. He stepped onto the field, the world narrowing to the ball at his feet. His chest felt tight, but with every step he took toward the goal, he reminded himself: *"This is for me."*

As he lined up for his first kick, Eli exhaled deeply, shutting out the noise, the doubt, and the fear. When his foot connected with the ball, it felt like a burst of energy—a release of all the tension he'd been carrying. The ball soared into the net.

For a moment, the gym was silent, the kind of silence that feels like it stretches forever.

Eli turned, his heart still racing, and saw the faces of his classmates—some surprised, others smiling. For the first time, he didn't feel like they were judging him. They were seeing him—not as the clumsy kid who stayed in the background, but as someone who belonged there.

Then, the applause began. It started softly, like a single drop of rain, then swelled into a thunderous wave that filled the gym. Eli blinked, his chest heaving as he stood frozen in place. For a moment, he couldn't believe what he was hearing. The faces turned toward him weren't mocking or disapproving. They were smiling, clapping—not judging, not laughing—just appreciating.

He had done it. The realization struck him like a jolt of sunlight after a cold, gray morning. He had faced his fears, stepped into the spotlight, and let himself be seen—not as the boy who tried to fade into the background, but as someone who had something worth sharing. And they had seen him, really seen him, for who he was.

Coach Miller stood near the edge of the court, his arms crossed, a proud grin spreading across his face. Eli met his gaze and, for the first time, didn't look away in doubt. Instead, he smiled—a real, unguarded smile.

"*I knew you had it in you,*" Coach said as Eli stepped off the court, his legs still shaky from the adrenaline rushing through him.

Eli managed a laugh, his voice steadier than he expected. "*I wasn't sure I did,*" he admitted. "*But once I got out there, it wasn't about them anymore. It was just about me and the game.*"

Coach nodded, his grin softening into something more thoughtful. "*That's the secret, Eli. It's always been about playing for yourself— not for anyone else's approval.*"

The next morning, Eli walked through the school hallway, the familiar buzz of chatter and slamming lockers all around him. But something was different. The noise didn't press down on him like it usually did. He didn't keep his eyes glued to the floor or try to squeeze past unnoticed. Instead, he walked with his head held high, his confidence quiet but steady.

"*Hey, Eli!*" a voice called out. He turned to see Max, a boy from his math class, jogging to catch up with him. "*That was awesome yesterday! I didn't know you could play like that.*"

Eli felt a warmth spread through his chest, not just from the compliment but from the realization that he didn't feel invisible anymore—and he was okay with that. "*Thanks,*" Eli said, his voice filled with genuine appreciation. "*It felt good to finally just go for it.*"

Max grinned, a little shy but clearly impressed. "*I wish I could be that brave. I'd be too scared to mess up in front of everyone.*"

Eli paused, considering his words carefully. "*You know,*" he began, "*I didn't feel brave at first. I was terrified. But sometimes, being brave doesn't mean you're not scared. It just means doing it anyway because it matters to you.*"

Max looked thoughtful, and Eli could see the spark of hope in his eyes—the same spark Coach Miller had lit in him. "*Maybe... maybe I'll try something like that someday.*"

Eli nodded, a sense of purpose blooming within him. "*And when you do, I'll be there to cheer you on.*"

As Max walked away, Eli lingered in the hallway for a moment, letting everything that had happened sink in. He wasn't the same boy who had tried to disappear at the start of the year. He had changed, grown—not just in how he saw himself, but in how he saw the world around him.

The hallway, once filled with obstacles and fear, now felt open and full of possibilities. Eli took a deep breath, feeling the steady rhythm of his heart, and realized he had finally found something greater than courage: a belief in himself.

Learning Lessons from "Finding His Courage"

Eli's journey highlights that courage isn't about being fearless—it's about taking action despite the fear. Boys often feel pressured to appear brave, but this story reframes bravery as embracing vulnerability and taking risks for things that matter to them.

Eli learns that his value doesn't come from being the best or meeting others' standards. His story reinforces the idea that self-worth comes from within, a lesson that resonates with boys who may struggle with comparisons in competitive environments.

Coach Miller's encouragement underscores the importance of having someone believe in you. This reflects the value of mentors in young boys' lives, teaching them that support can help them overcome self-doubt.

By stepping forward and finding his courage, Eli becomes a source of inspiration for Max, showing how one person's bravery can ripple outward and encourage others.

Story 2 - More Than Enough

The early morning sunlight filtered through the blinds, casting soft lines across Ben's bedroom. He blinked his eyes open, the familiar knot settling in his stomach before he even swung his legs out of bed. His hand instinctively reached for his tablet on the nightstand, fingers brushing its smooth surface.

"*Another day. Another reminder that I'm not good enough,*" Ben thought as he powered it on, his thumbs moving automatically to scroll through the endless feed of videos and highlights. Perfect trick shots. Flawless plays. Guys his age dunking basketballs, hitting impossible goals, or acing the latest video game challenges with thousands of likes and comments cheering them on.

Ben's gaze lingered on a video of a kid his age sinking a three-pointer from what looked like halfway across the court. The shot was in slow motion, the crowd cheering as the boy's confident smile filled the frame. "W*hy can't I do stuff like that?*" Ben wondered, his stomach tightening.

He knew, deep down, that some of these videos were edited, practiced over and over again to look effortless. But it didn't matter. All he could see was perfection. Each swipe reminded him of how far he was from being that good. It was like the screen in his hands was draining the color from his own world, making everything he tried seem smaller, less impressive.

With a frustrated sigh, Ben tossed the tablet onto his bed and walked over to the corner of his room where his basketball ball sat. He picked it up, turning it over in his hands. His fingers traced the worn seams, but instead of feeling inspired, he felt weighed down.

"*Why do I always feel like I'm not enough?*" The thought whispered through his mind like an echo, one that never seemed to fade.

"*I'm never going to be like them,*" he thought, glancing at the mirror across the room. His reflection stared back at him—someone caught between wanting to disappear and wishing he could stand out. He spun the basketball ball slowly, his eyes narrowing at the uneven stitching on one of the seams.

"*No matter what I do, I can't seem to get it right,*" he thought. His mind ran through the list of mistakes from the last basketball game at school—the passes he missed, the shot he hesitated on, the way Daniel, the team captain, always seemed to do it better.

The longer he held the ball, the heavier it seemed to get. Ben's shoulders sagged, and he let the basketball ball drop to the floor with a dull thud. "*Why even try?*"

It wasn't just the highlight reels online. It was the feeling that everyone else seemed to have it figured out—being better, faster, more confident. Meanwhile, he felt like he was stuck in place, always just missing the mark.

A soft knock sounded on his door. "*Ben?*" It was his older brother, Jason, poking his head in. "*You alright? You've been in here a while.*"

Ben quickly turned away from the mirror, rubbing at his eyes with the sleeve of his hoodie. *"Yeah, just… looking at stuff."*

Jason stepped into the room, his gaze landing on the tablet lying on Ben's bed and the basketball ball rolling slowly against the baseboard. He didn't have to ask to know what was going through Ben's mind. He'd been there before.

"You know…" Jason began gently, sitting on the edge of Ben's bed, *"I used to waste so much time watching those highlight reels, thinking if I could just pull off a trick shot like that, I'd finally feel good about myself."*

Ben looked over at his brother, his throat tight. *"And… did it work?"*

Jason smiled, a knowing kind of smile. *"Not even a little. I realized I was chasing something that wasn't even real. Most of the time, those videos are edited or staged. And even when they're not, they only show the moments people want you to see. You're comparing yourself to someone else's best moment."*

Jason leaned forward, his voice steady. *"You're more than just one shot or one game, Ben. You've got this way of seeing the game differently, making plays that no one else can. You can't measure yourself by someone else's highlight reel. That's not the whole story."*

Ben sat down next to Jason, his mind racing. *"Could it really be that simple? That the problem wasn't me?"* he wondered. He wanted to believe it, wanted to think that he didn't have to be perfect to be good enough. But the doubt clung to him, like a shadow he couldn't shake.

"But what if I mess up? What if I never get to that level?" Ben asked quietly, the frustration clear in his voice.

Jason reached out, resting a hand on Ben's shoulder. *"You're not supposed to be like them. You're supposed to be you. And the way you play, the way you think about the game—that's what makes you stand out. You've just gotta believe that's enough."*

"But how do I stop feeling like this? How do I stop comparing myself to them when it's everywhere I look?"

Jason reached out, placing a firm but gentle hand on Ben's shoulder. *"It starts with believing that you're enough, exactly as you are. No highlights, no replays. Just you."*

As Jason left the room, Ben glanced at the basketball ball resting by the wall. The weight of his tablet seemed to call out to him from the bed. It would've been so easy to pick it up again—to scroll, compare, and sink back into that spiral of doubt. But for the first time in a long while, Ben felt a flicker of something different. "*Maybe Jason's right,*" he thought. "*Maybe there's more to me than I've been letting myself see.*"

Ben crossed the room, hesitating for a moment before picking up the basketball ball. His reflection in the mirror still looked the same—unsure, caught between frustration and hope—but now, there was something else, too. A quiet strength, one he hadn't noticed before.

He bounced the ball once, the sound sharp and grounding. He wasn't sure if he believed everything Jason had said yet, but for the first time, he felt like he might be willing to try.

That morning, Ben left the tablet on his bed and walked out of his room, the basketball ball tucked under his arm. He wasn't sure what would come next, but maybe that was okay. Maybe figuring it out was part of the journey.

The next day, the familiar echo of sneakers squeaking on tile floors and the chatter of students filled the school hallways. Ben weaved through the crowd, the energy buzzing around him. The noise of the day felt distant, almost muted, as he made his way to class, his thoughts tangled in Jason's words.

He sat at his desk, staring at a blank notebook. The soft hum of conversation drifted from the hallway, but it barely registered. Jason's voice replayed in his head.

"You're comparing yourself to an illusion."

It had sounded so simple when Jason said it, but letting go of the comparisons wasn't easy. Every time Ben thought about the last game or glanced at someone's highlight video, the doubts crept back in, pulling him into the same loop of self-judgment.

His eyes flicked to his tablet, its screen dark in his backpack. It felt like a silent challenge, daring him to pick it up.

"What if I never feel like I'm enough? What if this feeling never goes away, no matter what I do?" The thought sat heavily in his chest.

He looked around the classroom. A group of boys in the corner were laughing about something. A few others were tapping away on their phones, showing off clips or memes. Every movement seemed so effortless, as if they weren't carrying the same weight that Ben was.

Ben shifted in his seat, tugging at the hem of his hoodie to cover his hands, almost as if hiding part of himself would make him invisible.

The classroom door swung open, and their teacher stepped in, her voice cutting through Ben's haze. *"Alright, everyone, put your phones away. I've got a new project for you."*

Ben barely listened as she started explaining, something about creating a personal project that highlighted their strengths— something unique about each student.

But when the teacher mentioned that these projects would be presented at the school's upcoming talent showcase, Ben's stomach twisted. The idea of standing up in front of everyone, putting himself out there for everyone to see, made his palms sweat.

The teacher continued, *"Think about what makes you. What are you passionate about? What's something that makes you unique?"*

Ben's thoughts spiraled. *"What if I don't have anything that makes me unique? What if I'm just... ordinary?"* The word stung in his mind, leaving an ache behind it. He'd spent so long trying to fit into the mold, trying to play like the best guys on the team, that he didn't even know where to start.

He flipped his pencil over and over in his hands, chewing on the edge of the eraser as doubts swirled in his head.

Later that afternoon, Ben slumped at the kitchen table at home, idly bouncing his basketball ball under the table with one hand. He hadn't even realized he was doing it until Jason walked in. Ben quickly grabbed the ball, holding it in his lap as if the act itself could erase the weight of his thoughts.

Jason raised an eyebrow but didn't say anything at first. Instead, he grabbed a bottle of water from the fridge and leaned against the counter. *"You look like something's on your mind,"* Jason said, his tone easy but curious.

Ben sighed, letting the ball roll a few inches across the table before catching it again. *"We got this project today. We're supposed to show what makes us unique, something we're passionate about, but... I don't even know what to do. Everyone else seems to know who they are, but I... don't."*

Jason frowned thoughtfully for a moment, then a small smile crept onto his face. *"Ben, you've always had this incredible way of reading the game. I've seen it—you see plays and make moves before anyone else. Why not start there?"*

Ben hesitated. *"You mean... talk about basketball? Everyone knows I play, but I'm not even the best at it."*

Jason shook his head. *"No, not just playing. I'm talking about how you see the game. The way you think about strategy, the way you break it down. That's your thing, Ben. That's what makes you stand out."*

Ben chewed on his lip, the idea rolling around in his mind. *"But what if they don't get it? What if it's not good enough?"*

Jason smiled gently, leaning forward. *"It's yours. That's what makes it special. It's not about whether they get it. It's about showing them how you see the game. Maybe it's time you let people see that part of you."*

That night, Ben sat at his desk with his basketball ball resting beside him. The same blank notebook from earlier stared back at him, its lines still waiting to be filled. This time, though, he flipped to a fresh page and began sketching out plays and diagrams, marking key moments from games he'd analyzed and ones he wanted to recreate.

As he worked, he added notes—little strategies and ideas he'd had while watching games on TV or practicing on his own. Each line of text felt like a piece of himself he was finally putting on paper.

"Maybe this is who I am. Maybe this is what makes me unique." He swallowed hard, feeling that familiar flutter of nerves in his stomach, but there was also something else—something lighter. Hope.

Ben kept sketching and writing, not for anyone else this time, but for himself. He wasn't sure how people would react, and the uncertainty still scared him. But for the first time, it didn't seem to matter as much. What mattered was that he was finally putting something real, something honest, into the world.

A week later, the school's annual talent showcase arrived faster than Ben expected. The event was no longer just an abstract thought—it was now very real. With every passing day, Ben had worked on his project, refining his diagrams, rehearsing how he'd explain his ideas, and even practicing in front of the mirror.

His nerves grew as the showcase day neared, but alongside the anxiety, he felt something else: determination.

On the day of the event, Ben stood behind the curtain, clutching his notebook filled with diagrams and notes. His hands trembled slightly, but he tightened his grip on the cover. There was no turning back.

"This is my moment," he thought.

Ben stood on the edge of the court, his heart pounding as he scanned the crowd of faces staring back at him. The gym lights were bright, almost too bright, and the hum of the packed bleachers buzzed in his ears. The school's talent showcase had always been something he avoided—a place where students put themselves out there, judged not only by what they could do but also by how effortlessly they seemed to pull it off.

But this year was different.

In his hands, he clutched his notebook, worn from being flipped through countless times, the pages covered in diagrams and notes about plays and strategies. It wasn't just a playbook anymore—it was his story. The thing Jason had encouraged him to share. The part of himself he'd kept private, thinking it didn't matter or wasn't enough.

"I can't believe I'm actually doing this," Ben thought, his breath coming faster as his nerves tightened with each passing second. *"What if they don't get it? What if they think it's stupid?"*

His mind flashed back to all the times he'd stood on the sidelines, second-guessing every move, comparing himself to Daniel or the others who always seemed to shine brighter on the court. He thought about how he'd hidden parts of himself—his ideas, his instincts—because he was afraid they wouldn't measure up.

But the truth was, he was done hiding.

"I've spent so much time trying to play like someone else," Ben thought, gripping the edges of the notebook tighter. *"This is me. This is how I see the game. This is what I have to offer."*

The murmurs from the crowd faded as the teacher stepped forward with the microphone. *"Next, we have Ben Carter, who will be presenting something very unique: his take on basketball strategy."*

Ben's stomach flipped as every pair of eyes turned to him. This was it. No hype, no fancy tricks—just him, standing in front of his peers, vulnerable and real. He could feel his hands trembling slightly, but he wasn't turning back now.

Jason's words echoed in his mind like a steadying mantra.

"Your perspective matters, Ben. You matter. Don't be afraid to show the world who you really are."

That final push was all he needed. Ben took a deep breath and stepped into the center of the court. His heart raced, but as he opened the notebook, the familiar diagrams and notes staring back at him, something inside him steadied.

The first words from Ben's notebook escaped his lips quietly, his voice shaky at first but growing steadier with each sentence. This time, he wasn't holding back. Ben explained the strategy he'd drawn up, his eyes scanning the court as he spoke.

He described the plays he'd imagined, the way the team could shift together to create space, the opportunities he saw in moments others might overlook.

He wasn't just sharing his plays—he was sharing the way he saw the game. Not just for himself, but for anyone who'd ever felt like their voice didn't matter:

"The game isn't just about speed or strength.
It's about the patterns you see, the chances you take.
It's about reading the court,
Even when others can't see what you do.
It's not about being flashy or loud,
It's about the quiet moves that set things in motion.
It's about trusting yourself,
Even when others might not see your worth.
The court doesn't care if you're perfect.
It's about how you show up,
How you give everything to the team.
And that's what makes you enough."

Ben's voice carried across the gym, filling the silence as the vulnerability in his words hung in the air. With each idea he shared, he felt himself standing a little taller, his voice growing stronger.

As he explained the final play, Ben realized something: he wasn't scared anymore. He wasn't presenting for their approval. He was sharing a part of himself—his truth—and it didn't matter how they reacted.

"For so long, I thought I had to play like someone else to matter. But this, right here, is what's real. This is me."

A calm washed over him, and for the first time, Ben felt free. He wasn't hiding behind comparisons, trying to measure up to someone else's game. He was standing in his own truth, and that was enough.

The gym was still for a moment after he finished. Then, slowly, applause began to build. At first, it was polite, but it grew louder, stronger. Ben blinked, looking out at the faces in the crowd. Some looked surprised, others intrigued. But most of all, they weren't dismissing him. They weren't mocking him. They were just... listening.

"They're listening to me," Ben thought, his chest swelling with pride. *"Not because I'm the best on the team, but because I have something to say."*

As he stepped off the court, Jason was waiting for him by the bleachers, grinning wide. *"You crushed it, Ben."*

Ben smiled back, a real smile this time. *"Thanks. It felt... good."* He let out a deep breath, the tension melting away. *"Really good."*

Jason nodded, his eyes filled with pride. *"See? I told you, Ben. You've always had this in you."*

Ben glanced back at the court, then at his brother. He had crossed a threshold tonight—not just in sharing his ideas, but in believing in himself. He had returned to the team, not as the kid who doubted every move he made, but as someone who finally trusted his own instincts, his own perspective.

"This is me. I'm not perfect, but I'm more than enough. I've always been more than enough."

Learning Lessons from "More Than Enough"

Ben's journey reminds boys that their value isn't defined by how they measure up to others on the court, online, or anywhere else. It's easy to fall into the trap of comparison, thinking you need to be the fastest, strongest, or most popular to matter. But true strength comes from recognizing what makes you unique and trusting that it's enough.

Jason's guidance highlights a critical truth: self-acceptance begins with letting go of the need to perform for others. You don't have to be the best to be valuable—you already are. Your quirks, your ideas, your quiet strengths are all part of what makes you who you are.

Ben's decision to share his ideas teaches that courage isn't the absence of fear—it's choosing to show up anyway. By stepping into the spotlight and sharing his authentic self, Ben not only found his voice but also inspired others to see the game—and themselves—in a new way.

Your perspective matters. Your uniqueness is your power. And no matter what the world says, you are more than enough—always have been, always will be.

Story 3 - Sketching Strength

The morning light filtered through the half-closed blinds of Ethan's room, casting faint lines across his desk, where crumpled sketches and half-finished doodles littered the surface. He lay still in bed, staring at the ceiling, feeling that same heavy weight in his chest—one he had grown used to.

He sighed, pulling the blanket over his head as if it could shield him from the day ahead.

His phone buzzed on the nightstand, breaking the silence. Without thinking, he reached for it, the cool glass screen smooth beneath his fingertips. Checking social media was a habit—one he didn't even enjoy anymore, but one he couldn't seem to stop.

His thumb scrolled absently, passing highlight reels of classmates— guys scoring impossible goals, flashing perfect smiles, or making ridiculous trick shots look effortless. They made everything seem so easy. So effortless.

"Why does it always feel so easy for them?" Ethan thought, a familiar knot tightening in his stomach. *"Why do they always look so... sure of themselves?"*

He stopped at a photo of a group of boys from school. No one was showing off, no one was posing—but still, they looked cool. Confident. Like they belonged.

Ethan's eyes flickered toward the reflection in the mirror across the room, and his stomach sank. Baggy hoodie, messy hair, and dark circles under his eyes from sketching too late the night before. It was like looking at someone who didn't fit anywhere. Someone who wasn't enough.

He looked away. He hated mirrors.

At school, the day dragged on like any other. Ethan kept his head down, staying quiet, blending in. He sat in the back of the classroom, his notebook open—but untouched.

The hum of voices from his classmates surrounded him, but he felt distant, like he was watching from the outside.

Then, the teacher's voice cut through the noise. "Alright, class. We're starting a new project—something personal. I want each of you to create something that represents who you are, something unique to you."

Ethan's pulse quickened. *"Something that represents me?"*

His mind raced, but all he found was doubt. *"What do I have to show? What's so special about me?"*

The idea of creating something personal terrified him. He wasn't like the other guys. He didn't have crazy soccer skills like Aaron, couldn't land skateboard tricks like Marcus, and wasn't the guy cracking jokes in the middle of class like Jake.

What did he have that made him stand out?

Apparently for Ethan: *"Nothing."*

As soon as the class ended, Ethan stuffed his notebook into his bag and bolted for the door, his hands gripping the straps of his backpack so tightly his knuckles turned white.

"I can't do this," he thought, dodging students in the hallway. *"I don't even know who I am, let alone what makes me special."*

For the rest of the day, the project haunted him. Every time he thought about it, his brain filled with images of his classmates—guys who knew who they were, who were good at things that mattered.

And then there was him: just some kid who liked to sketch in the margins of his notebook.

That night, back in the quiet of his bedroom, Ethan paced the floor, frustration bubbling up inside him. He hated this feeling. This stupid, nagging thought that he wasn't enough.

He could just ignore the project. Fake his way through it, turn in something simple and meaningless. That would be easier than showing people how lost he really felt.

But deep down, that idea scared him even more.

A soft knock came from his door. *"Ethan?"* He froze. It was Leo, his older cousin, who had been crashing at their house for a few weeks.

Ethan hesitated, but eventually, he cracked the door open, allowing Leo to step inside.

Leo was everything Ethan wasn't—confident, laid-back, the kind of guy who seemed at home anywhere. Ethan had always looked up to him, even if he didn't always understand how Leo made things look so easy.

But tonight, something felt different. Leo wasn't here to crack a joke or ruffle Ethan's hair. He sat down on the edge of the bed, glancing around at the scattered sketches on Ethan's desk.

"What's going on, man?" Leo asked, his voice calm.

Ethan wasn't sure how to put it into words. Finally, he mumbled, *"We got this project at school. Something about showing who we are, but... I don't think I can do it."*

Leo raised an eyebrow, intrigued. *"Why not?"*

Ethan looked down at his hands, fingers fidgeting with the hem of his hoodie. *"Because I don't know who I am. I'm... I'm nothing special. I don't have that confidence like you. I don't have anything worth showing."*

Leo exhaled, leaning forward with a small smile. *"You think I've always been like this?"*

Ethan glanced up. Leo was the guy who could talk to anyone, who seemed comfortable in any situation. He made confidence look easy.

Leo tapped his fingers against the desk. *"I used to think the same thing. That I had nothing to offer. That I'd always be the kid no one noticed. But confidence doesn't come from being like everyone else, man. It comes from accepting what makes you different."*

Ethan frowned. *"But... what if they don't get it? What if I put myself out there and they just think I'm a joke?"*

Leo placed a hand on Ethan's shoulder. *"Trust me, kid. You are far from ordinary. You've got something unique—you just have to start seeing it."*

That night, Ethan lay in bed, staring at the ceiling. Leo's words replayed in his mind: *"It's time you start seeing that."*

Could it really be that simple? That maybe, just maybe, he had something worth showing?

He turned over, burying his face in his pillow. He could play it safe—turn in some generic project, something easy. Stay invisible.

Or...

He could take a risk.

The thought sent a nervous jolt through him, but somewhere beneath that fear, a tiny flicker of excitement stirred.

Ethan sat up, reached under his bed, and pulled out his sketchbook. Slowly, hesitantly, he began to draw.

Maybe, he thought as the first lines formed beneath his pencil, *"Maybe there's more to me than I've been willing to see."*

He wasn't sure where this was leading. But for the first time, he was willing to take the first step.

The next morning, Ethan walked into school with his sketchbook tucked tightly under his arm.

The familiar hum of students moving through the halls filled the air—lockers slamming shut, sneakers scuffing against the floors, laughter echoing from different groups.

Ethan kept his head down, weaving through the crowded hallway, heading toward his usual spot in the cafeteria—near the back, where he could be alone.

He sat down, opening his sketchbook to the drawing he had worked on the night before. He had spent hours sketching—pouring his thoughts, his hopes, and his fears into the art.

But now, in the harsh light of the cafeteria, his confidence was unraveling.

"What if it's not good enough?"

Doubt crept in like a slow-moving tide. What if his sketches weren't impressive? What if people just thought they were dumb?

He glanced up at his classmates—guys cracking jokes, showing off ridiculous trick shots on their phones, tossing crumpled napkins into the trash like basketballs.

And then there were the kids he avoided—the ones who always had something to say.

Ethan tensed as he spotted them across the room. His stomach twisted.

Instinctively, he hunched over his sketchbook, pulling his hoodie tighter around him, like a shield. He just had to keep his head down, stay unnoticed.

But one of them caught his eye. A smirk spread across his face.

"Still hiding behind that sketchbook, Ethan?" The words cut through the cafeteria noise, loud enough for the surrounding tables to hear.

Ethan's heart pounded.

Laughter followed.

Each chuckle was like a sharp pin pricking his confidence. His face burned. His hands clenched around his pencil.

"Why can't I be like them? Why am I always the target?"

For a moment, the weight of self-doubt threatened to crush him.

Before Ethan could retreat into himself, he felt a presence beside him. It was Noah, his friend—the one who never liked attention but always had Ethan's back in small, quiet ways.

But today was different.

"*Hey, back off,*" Noah said, his voice steady. His words weren't loud, but they were firm enough to cut through the laughter.

The bullies exchanged glances, snickering under their breath. But they didn't push further. The cafeteria noise swallowed their comments as they moved on.

Ethan blinked in surprise, his heart still racing. "*You didn't have to do that,*" he muttered, feeling embarrassed by the attention.

Noah shrugged. "*I know. But you shouldn't have to deal with them alone.*"

Ethan didn't know what to say. He had spent so long thinking he was in this by himself—that no one really saw him.

But maybe Noah was right. Maybe he didn't have to go through this alone.

Later that afternoon, Ethan found himself standing in front of the classroom door. Inside, students were setting up their projects, chatting, adjusting posters, and flipping through notebooks.

His stomach churned. The fear of putting himself out there wrapped around him like a rope, tightening its grip.

He could turn around.

No one would blame him if he just skipped the presentation.

But deep down, Ethan knew he had come to a point where he needed to face this head-on. He couldn't keep hiding.

Leo's words echoed in his mind:

"You've got more going on than you give yourself credit for. It's time you start seeing that."

Ethan inhaled sharply, gripping the strap of his backpack.

He pushed open the door and stepped inside.

The low buzz of voices seemed to fade as he walked to his seat, pulling out his sketchbook. His hands trembled.

Was he really about to do this?

When it was Ethan's turn, the silence in the classroom felt heavier than ever. He stood at the front of the room, heart pounding so loudly it drowned out everything else.

His fingers clutched the edge of his sketchbook. His legs felt stiff. His mind raced.

"What if they laugh? What if they don't get it?". But there was no turning back now.

Slowly, he flipped open his sketchbook.

On the page was a drawing—not of superheroes or fantasy worlds, but of himself.

It wasn't perfect. The lines were rough, unpolished. But it was real. It showed him as he was, not how he wished he could be.

Somehow, he had managed to capture the way he felt when he thought no one saw him. The way he always stayed in the background, watching, listening, waiting for the moment he could just blend in.

His voice felt dry when he spoke. But then, the words started coming.

"*I... I wanted to draw something real.*" His voice was shaky at first, but with every word, it steadied. "*I've spent so long trying to stay invisible. Not because I wanted to be, but because I thought that was easier. But this is me. And I'm starting to think maybe... maybe that's okay.*"

His words hung in the air.

For a long second, no one said anything. And then, someone clapped.

Soft at first. Then another. Until the entire room filled with applause.

Ethan's breath caught in his throat. They weren't laughing. They weren't judging. They were just... listening. They saw him.

As Ethan sat back down, his heart still racing, Noah leaned over with a small smile.

"*That was awesome, man. You're awesome!*". Ethan didn't know what to say. But for the first time, he believed it.

Ethan didn't know how to respond at first. He felt lighter, freer than he had in a long time.

For the first time, he hadn't been hiding behind his hoodie or his silence. He had shared something real—a part of himself—and it had been enough.

And maybe, just maybe, he could keep doing that.

Because he was learning that who he was... was already enough.

The school bell rang, signaling the end of the day. Students trickled out of the building, voices blending together, sneakers squeaking against the tiled floors.

Ethan stood near the door, heart still buzzing from the presentation.

He had done it.

He had stood up there in front of everyone, let them see a side of him they'd never seen before, and he had survived.

As the hall emptied, he stepped outside, the cool evening air brushing against his skin.

The sun was setting, stretching shadows across the sidewalk as he walked home, his sketchbook tucked securely under his arm.

The applause from earlier still echoed in his head—a distant reminder of the courage it had taken to stand up there. At first, he had expected to feel relief, like finishing a hard test or escaping an awkward situation. But now, as he walked, a different thought crept in.

"What now?"

The thrill of the moment was fading, replaced by lingering doubt. Did any of this change how he felt about himself?

Ethan stopped in front of a store window, his reflection caught in the glass.

For a second, he saw the kid he used to be—the one who kept his head down, who barely spoke up, who thought it was safer to stay invisible.

Then, a different memory surfaced—the way he had stood in front of the class, the way his voice had steadied, the way people had actually listened.

His reflection looked different now—more familiar, less like a stranger.

The old doubts were still there, but they didn't feel so heavy anymore. There was something new—a quiet strength, the beginnings of acceptance.

The next morning, Ethan stood at his locker, pulling out his books.

He wasn't expecting to face the same group of guys who had messed with him before. But there they were—leaning against the lockers, laughing, exchanging smug looks.

For a brief moment, the old fear returned.

The instinct to lower his gaze, to keep his head down, to shrink back into the background.

"You're not ready for this," the voice in his head whispered. *"Nothing's really changed."*

But then... he remembered.

He remembered standing in the classroom, the way his voice had risen, the way the applause had felt like an acknowledgment of something deeper than his art.

And he remembered Leo's words: *"Confidence doesn't come from trying to be like everyone else. It comes from owning what makes you different."*

Ethan straightened his back. He didn't need to say anything to them. He didn't need their approval.

Instead, he simply met their eyes as they passed. His expression wasn't angry or afraid—it was calm. Unshaken. They don't define me, Ethan thought. I know who I am now.

The guys kept walking, their laughter fading into the distance.

And for the first time, Ethan didn't feel small in their presence. He didn't feel the need to disappear. He felt free.

That afternoon, Ethan found himself back in the art room. It was quiet, the scent of paint and pencil shavings filling the air. He sat down, flipping through his sketchbook. He thought about how far he had come.

His self-portrait was still imperfect, still raw. But now, it felt like a reflection of his journey, not his flaws.

And that?

That was enough.

Just as Ethan was about to pack up his sketchbook, he noticed a younger boy lingering by the art room door. The kid looked hesitant, his fingers gripping the edges of a drawing that was crumpled from being held too tightly.

Ethan recognized that look instantly—it was the same fear he had once felt. The fear of putting something personal out there and having it torn down.

He took a step forward. *"Hey,"* he said, keeping his voice casual. *"Whatcha got there?"*

The kid shifted, eyes darting toward the floor. *"It's just... something I was working on. But it's not that good."*

Ethan smiled, feeling a strange sense of familiarity in the moment. *"Can I see?"*

The kid hesitated, but after a moment, he held out the paper. The drawing was rough, full of scribbled lines and shaky strokes—but it had something. Something real.

Ethan studied it for a second, then nodded. *"This is awesome."* He handed it back. *"You've got talent, man."*

The boy blinked up at him. *"You really think so?"*

Ethan nodded again. "*Yeah. Don't be afraid to share it. People will see the heart in your work—just like I did.*"

The kid's grip on the drawing loosened slightly. For the first time, Ethan saw a flicker of belief in his expression. And in that moment, Ethan realized something.

He wasn't just helping someone else—he was seeing just how far he had come himself.

As Ethan stepped out of the art room, the warm glow of the late afternoon sun streamed through the windows.

He felt lighter. His insecurities hadn't vanished, and they probably never would. But that was okay.

Because now he understood something far more important—

His worth had never been about how others saw him. It had never been about whether he fit in or stayed invisible. His worth had been there all along. And now, he finally believed it.

And that was the real reward.

Learning Lessons from "Sketching Strength"

Ethan's story shows you that true confidence isn't about being perfect—it's about owning who you are, flaws and all. The path to self-acceptance begins when you stop comparing yourself to others and start appreciating your own unique strengths.

Just like Ethan discovered through his art, your imperfections are part of what make you real, relatable, and strong.

Comparison is a trap. Ethan learned that the people who matter most aren't the ones judging you from a distance—they're the ones who see your heart, your effort, and your courage.

Courage doesn't mean never being afraid—it means stepping forward even when you are.

By sharing his self-portrait, Ethan found the strength to stand in his truth—not for approval, but for himself. And in doing so, he inspired others. Let Ethan's story remind you:

You are enough as you are.

Your voice, your talents, and your story are worth sharing. And when you finally step forward, you'll realize just how much you've had inside you all along.

Story 4 - The Art of Being True

The day at Westbrook Middle School started like any other, but for Ryan, each morning felt like stepping onto a playing field where he was always on the bench.

As he walked through the hallways, he saw the usual groups—the star athletes, the confident guys who always knew what to say, the kids who fit in without trying.

Ryan wasn't one of them.

He wasn't the loudest, the strongest, or the funniest. He wasn't a class clown or a sports star. He loved drawing, but no one really knew that about him.

He tugged at the sleeves of his worn hoodie, his go-to outfit, his shield.

"If I could just change something—anything—maybe I'd fit in. Maybe they'd notice me."

He reached his locker just as the usual group of guys burst into laughter nearby. He wasn't sure if they were laughing at him or if he was just so used to feeling out of place that it didn't matter anymore.

Ryan slumped into his usual seat at the back of class.

The chatter of his classmates filled the room, but he kept his head down, absently sketching in his notebook—something he always did when he didn't want to be noticed.

Then, a voice cut through the noise.

"*Yo, Ryan.*"

Ryan glanced up. It was Luke, one of the most popular guys in school—captain of the soccer team, always surrounded by people, the kind of guy who never seemed unsure of himself.

Luke leaned back in his chair, grinning. "*You ever think about getting a new style?*"

Ryan blinked. "*Uh... what?*"

Luke motioned to Ryan's hoodie. "*I mean, no offense, but you've been wearing that thing since, like, forever.*"

Ryan shrugged, unsure where this was going.

"*Me and the guys are heading to the mall this weekend. You should come with us—maybe get something fresh, y'know? Change it up a little.*"

For a second, Ryan's heart jumped.

Was this it? His chance to fit in?

He could almost picture it—walking into school with Luke and the guys, cracking jokes, finally feeling like he belonged.

All he had to do was say yes. But as the vision played out in his mind, something twisted in his stomach.

"Would they actually accept me? Or am I just a project to them?"

He wasn't sure.

Later that afternoon, Ryan stood in front of his mirror at home.

Luke's words kept replaying in his head. *"Maybe a different look would help. Maybe I should try to stand out more."*

He looked down at his hoodie—his safest armor against judgment. He wasn't the kind of guy who cared about brands or trends.

His go-to outfits—graphic t-shirts, loose jeans, and sneakers that had seen better days—felt like him.

But... if changing meant fitting in, wasn't it worth considering?

"If I go with them, I'll have to change everything about myself. I don't know if I can do that."

He ran a hand through his hair, frustration bubbling inside him. *"But if I don't go, what if I miss my only shot at finally belonging?"*

That evening, Uncle Mark stopped by for dinner.

Ryan had always looked up to Mark—he wasn't flashy, wasn't the loudest guy in the room, but people respected him.

After dinner, Mark noticed Ryan staring off into space.

"You good, kid?"

Ryan hesitated but decided to be honest. He told Mark about the invitation, the pressure to change, the feeling of not being good enough.

Mark listened, then leaned back in his chair, thoughtful.

"Y'know, when I was your age, I tried to fit in with the 'cool guys' too. Thought if I could change a few things—my clothes, the way I talked— people would respect me more."

Ryan sat up, curious. *"Did it work?"*

Mark chuckled. *"For about two weeks."*

Ryan frowned. *"What happened?"*

Mark shrugged. *"I realized that no matter how much I changed, it was never gonna be enough for them. And in trying to impress them, I lost the things that actually made me happy."*

Ryan was quiet for a moment. *"So what did you do?"*

Mark smiled. "I stopped pretending. The right people—the ones who really matter—will like you for who you are, not who you're trying to be."

Ryan nodded slowly, but the question still gnawed at him - *"What if I never fit in? What if being myself isn't enough?"*

Later that night, Ryan lay awake in bed, staring at the ceiling. Mark's words echoed in his head: *"The right people will like you for who you are."*

Could it really be that simple?

He rolled over and grabbed his sketchbook from under his bed—his real safe space. For the first time in days, he let himself draw.

The pencil moved across the page, lines forming into something familiar—himself.

Not the version of him Luke wanted to see. Not the version that tried to be someone he wasn't. Just him.

And maybe—just maybe—that was enough.

The next day, as Ryan stood at his locker, he spotted Luke and his group further down the hall. They were laughing, tossing a football between them, looking like they belonged effortlessly.

Ryan felt that familiar tug of longing—to be included, to be noticed. But something inside him had shifted.

Luke's offer still echoed in his head: Come with us. Change it up. Fit in.

Ryan had made a decision. He would go to the mall with Luke and his friends, but he wasn't going to change himself completely just to fit in. He took a deep breath, squared his shoulders, and approached the group.

"Hey, about this weekend..." he started, keeping his voice casual. *"I'll come. But I'm not changing everything about myself. I like who I am."*

Luke blinked, caught off guard. A flicker of confusion crossed his face.

"Yeah, sure, man. Whatever you say."

Ryan wasn't sure if that was acceptance or just indifference, but for the first time, he felt a small spark of confidence—like he had taken a step closer to figuring out who he really was.

The weekend arrived faster than Ryan expected.

As he walked toward the mall, his mind swirled with a mix of anticipation and doubt.

He had promised himself he wouldn't change, but now, with every step closer, the pressure to conform felt heavier. He could already picture

Luke and the guys cracking jokes, testing him, waiting to see if he would go along with them.

Could he? Should he?

Ryan took a deep breath and stepped inside the store, instantly overwhelmed.

Rows of brand-name sneakers, racks of expensive jackets, shelves lined with the latest athletic gear—everything screamed status.

The kind of stuff guys like Luke wore. The kind of stuff Ryan never really cared about.

But here, it felt like a uniform—one he was expected to put on if he wanted in.

Luke walked ahead confidently, pulling a pair of high-end sneakers off the shelf and tossing them toward Ryan.

"Dude, these are sick. You should get 'em."

Ryan caught the shoes, turning them over in his hands.

They were nice, sure. But they weren't him.

"Uh... I dunno," Ryan muttered. *"They're kinda expensive."*

Luke smirked. *"Man, c'mon. You want people to notice you, right? This is how you do it."*

Ryan hesitated. That was exactly what he wanted, wasn't it?

To not feel invisible. To be seen as more than the quiet kid in the back, the one who never really stood out.

He looked at the shoes again.

They felt heavy in his hands—like a choice he wasn't sure he wanted to make.

Ryan glanced up, catching his reflection in the store's mirror.

There he was. Baggy hoodie, sneakers that were worn down but comfortable, jeans that were his, not something picked to impress others.

And then he pictured himself in the new shoes, wearing the same styles as Luke and his friends—walking into school looking like someone he wasn't.

Something about that felt wrong.

"Why am I doing this? To fit in? But at what cost?"

Ryan swallowed hard. Was he really willing to trade in the things that made him feel like himself just to belong?

Luke clapped a hand on Ryan's shoulder.

"Dude, just buy 'em. You wanna start looking the part, right?"

Ryan felt boxed in.

The guys were watching him, waiting.

His heart pounded in his chest. And before he could think—before he could even stop himself—he nodded.

"Yeah. Alright."

He handed over the money, feeling a strange heaviness settle over him as the cashier rang up the purchase.

The bag pressed against his side like a weight as he left the store.

And for the first time, Ryan wasn't sure if he had gained something...
or lost something.

The rest of the trip was a blur. Ryan followed along, nodding when the
others talked about sports, sneakers, and brands he had never cared
about before.

But his mind was elsewhere.

The more he tried to blend in, the more disconnected he felt from
himself.

By the time he got home, the weight of the day hung over him like a
heavy backpack he couldn't put down.

That night, Ryan sat at his desk, his sketchbook untouched.

He used to draw whenever his mind felt cluttered, letting his pencil
make sense of his thoughts. But lately, he hadn't drawn at all.

It was like trying to fit in with Luke's group had drained everything
that made him feel like himself.

His phone buzzed. A message from Luke: "*Can't wait to see you at
school tomorrow in those kicks! Time to show 'em what's up!*"

Ryan's stomach twisted.

The thought of walking into school, wearing those brand-new sneakers
that didn't feel like his, made him feel physically sick.

He stared at his phone screen, fingers hovering over the keyboard.

"*Do I even want this?*"

"*What am I trying to prove, and to whom?*"

The next morning, Ryan stood in front of the mirror. The reflection staring back at him felt... off.

The new sneakers—fresh, spotless, nothing like the worn-in pair he loved—stood out. They weren't him.

But there he was, wearing them anyway, about to walk out the door, feeling like an imposter in his own skin.

Ryan stepped into school, every step feeling heavier than the last.

Luke spotted him immediately, flashing a satisfied grin. *"There he is! Fresh kicks, bro. Told you it'd feel different, right?"*

Ryan forced a smile, but the unease only grew.

He caught glimpses of himself in the school's glass windows as he walked by, and with every glance, a pit of dread formed deeper in his chest.

By lunchtime, the pressure became unbearable.

He excused himself from the group and found a quiet spot outside, away from the crowd. He slumped against the wall, his chest tightening as the realization hit him like a weight he had been trying to ignore.

This wasn't who he was.

He had tried so hard to be someone else—but in doing so, he had lost himself.

His mind raced, replaying Uncle Mark's words from their conversation a few nights ago: *"The right people will like you for who you are, not who you pretend to be."*

And just like that, it all clicked.

He didn't need to be like Luke. He didn't need new sneakers to matter.

The real Ryan—the kid who sketched designs in his notebook, who wore beat-up sneakers because they had stories in them—was enough.

He always had been.

Ryan straightened, feeling a sense of clarity wash over him. He pulled his phone from his pocket and typed a message to Luke:

"I can't do this anymore. This isn't me."

His heart pounded as he hit send, but for the first time in weeks, he felt lighter.

When he got home, Ryan grabbed his sketchbook and flipped to a blank page. He picked up his pencil and began to draw.

The lines flowed effortlessly, like he was rediscovering a part of himself he had hidden away.

For the first time in a long while, he smiled. This was who he was. Not some guy trying to fit into Luke's world. Just Ryan—creative, independent, unique. And that was everything he needed to be.

It had been a few days since Ryan sent the message to Luke and made the decision to be himself again.

Now, as he walked through the halls of school—the same halls that had once felt like a battlefield—things felt different.

Lighter.

He wasn't hiding anymore.

Instead of keeping his head down or trying to blend in, he walked a little taller, his steps feeling more like his own.

But the road back to himself wasn't without its challenges.

As Ryan passed by Luke and the others, he braced himself for their reaction. Luke glanced his way, but this time, there was no grin, no head nod, no inside joke waiting for him.

Instead, there was indifference—a short glance, then nothing.

It was like he had disappeared from their radar completely. And somehow, that stung more than he had expected. For a moment, doubt flickered in his mind.

"Did I make the right choice?"

"Maybe I should've just gone along with it."

His stomach twisted as he quickened his pace. But as soon as the thought entered his mind, he shook it off.

No.

He had finally chosen his own path.

The road back wasn't about winning their approval. It was about finding peace with who he was.

Later that afternoon, Ryan sat in the school's art room, his sketchbook in hand.

The sound of pencil strokes against paper was calming, steady. This was his space. The place where he could think clearly, breathe freely, and express himself without judgment.

As he shaded in the final details of his drawing—a figure standing under an open sky, free, unburdened—he felt something new.

A sense of renewal. Like he was finally getting back to himself.

The quiet murmur of the art room surrounded him, grounding him in the moment.

A knock on the door interrupted his thoughts. Teacher Mark stepped in, a warm smile on his face.

"How's my favorite artist doing?" he asked, leaning against the doorway.

Ryan smiled, looking down at his drawing. *"Better. I think I'm finally figuring things out."*

Mark walked over, glancing at the sketchbook.

"You know," he said, his voice calm and steady, *"standing up for who you are—that's something a lot of people don't figure out. Not until much later."*

Ryan looked at Mark, feeling a swell of pride in his chest.

"It wasn't easy," he admitted, his voice quieter now.

"There are still moments where I wonder if I made the right choice... but I don't want to go back to pretending. I'm tired of being someone I'm not."

Mark nodded, placing a firm but reassuring hand on Ryan's shoulder.

"It takes time. But you're already so much stronger than you realize."

As Mark left, Ryan stared down at his sketch again.

His hand hovered over the page, adding a final detail—a beam of light breaking through stormy clouds.

It was more than just an image. It was him.

A reminder that he had risen above the pressure to fit in and found strength in being himself.

The day of Westbrook High's "Self-Expression Day" arrived faster than Ryan had expected.

It wasn't a talent show. It wasn't a competition. It was an opportunity— for students to showcase something meaningful to them, something that reflected who they truly were.

And for Ryan, it was exactly the kind of moment he needed.

This wasn't about proving himself. This was about owning who he was.

For himself.

His art had always been a part of him, something that helped him make sense of the world.

But today?

Today, he was ready to share it.

As students wandered through the gym-turned-gallery, Ryan stood next to his display — a sketch of a lone figure standing under an open sky, free from expectations.

The drawing told his story. The struggle of self-doubt. The weight of trying to fit in.

And finally...

The freedom of choosing his own path.

A small crowd started to gather, murmurs of admiration filling the space. And for the first time, Ryan wasn't nervous.

There was still that slight flutter in his chest, but it wasn't fear.

It was a quiet confidence—one he had never felt before.

A younger student approached, eyes locked on the sketch.

"*This is awesome,*" he said. "*It's like... I can feel what it means.*"

Ryan glanced at the kid—maybe a freshman, someone still trying to find his place.

He recognized that look. Because he had been there, too.

Ryan smiled, fingers brushing the edges of his sketchbook. "*It's how I express myself,*" he said, his voice steady.

"*I used to think I had to be like everyone else to fit in. But I've learned that it's okay to just be me. That's what this is about.*"

The kid nodded, staring at the drawing a little longer before walking away.

And in that moment, Ryan realized something.

This wasn't just about his journey. It was about helping others see that they didn't have to fit into anyone else's mold either.

As the event came to an end, Ryan stepped out of the gym. The weight of trying to conform had been lifted. Replaced by something stronger.

The certainty that he didn't need anyone else's approval to know his own worth. He had found his voice.

His confidence. His own identity. The elixir he had gained?

The quiet understanding that he was enough—just as he was.

Learning Lessons from "The Art of Being True"

You don't have to change who you are to belong.

Ryan's journey shows that real confidence doesn't come from blending in—it comes from embracing who you truly are.

At some point, you might feel pressure to fit in, to change the way you dress, talk, or act just to be accepted. But the truth is, changing yourself for others will never feel right if it means losing the things that make you, you.

Ryan thought fitting in meant changing himself to match what others expected. But he learned that pretending to be someone else feels empty, the right people will respect you for who you are and confidence comes from staying true to yourself.

It's okay to want to be liked. But real belonging doesn't come from impressing others—it comes from being yourself and finding people who appreciate you for it.

Ryan's story teaches us that self-acceptance is the key to real confidence. When you stop worrying about who you "should" be and start owning who you are, you feel more at peace and discover your strengths and what makes you unique. And that's what really matters.

Story 5 - This is me

The late afternoon sun streamed through the blinds, casting streaks of light across Liam's room. He sat at his desk, flipping a pencil between his fingers, staring down at a half-filled notebook.

Not that he was doing any homework.

The page in front of him was covered in random doodles of characters, sports logos, and rough sketches of sneakers—things he usually liked to draw. But today, nothing felt right.

His eyes kept drifting toward the open closet door, where a pile of clothes lay crumpled on the floor.

His favorite hoodie—the one he'd worn almost every day last year—felt too tight now, the sleeves shorter than they should be. Even his jeans weren't fitting the same anymore.

Liam exhaled sharply.

"Why does everything feel weird all of a sudden?"

Lately, his body was changing, and he wasn't sure how to feel about it. His shoulders were broader, but he wasn't as tall as some of his friends. He was gaining muscle, but not enough to look like the guys on his soccer team. He just felt... stuck.

His phone buzzed. Probably his friends in the group chat, talking about meeting up at the park this weekend.

Liam ignored it.

Instead, his gaze flicked toward the mirror hanging on the wall.

He hesitated.

He used to not care about his reflection, but now, every time he looked, he felt... off. Like his body was changing without him having any say in it.

He stole a quick glance—just for a second—but it was enough.

He didn't like what he saw.

His arms weren't quite strong enough. His face didn't look the same as it used to. Even his jawline seemed different.

Annoyed, Liam yanked his hoodie off the floor and tossed it over the mirror.

Problem solved.

At dinner, the usual chaos filled the kitchen. His little brother, Noah, was going on and on about a new video game. His mom was asking how school went.

Liam barely paid attention.

He could feel his shirt clinging in a way that didn't feel right.

And then, his mom dropped the bomb. *"Liam, we're going shopping this weekend. You could use some new clothes."*

Liam nearly dropped his fork.

Shopping?

Trying things on?

Standing in front of a mirror with a million lights pointing at him?

Nope.

His stomach twisted, and suddenly, he wasn't hungry anymore.

"Do I have to?" he muttered, avoiding eye contact. His mom gave him a knowing look. *"You'll feel better in clothes that actually fit."*

Yeah, right.

She didn't get it.

She didn't understand that shopping meant facing something he was trying to avoid.

That night, Liam lay in bed, staring at the ceiling.

Shopping wasn't the problem. It was what it meant. It meant standing in front of a mirror under the bright, unforgiving lights. It meant realizing his body had changed—and that he had no control over it.

He rolled over, pulling his blanket tighter.

"What if I never feel comfortable in my own skin again?" The thought sat heavy in his chest, making it hard to breathe. He had always assumed growing up would feel different.

Cooler. But right now, it just felt awkward and wrong.

The next morning, after breakfast, Liam's older cousin, Jake, dropped by unexpectedly. Jake was in college now. Confident. Athletic. The kind of guy who made everything look easy.

They sat in the living room, half-watching TV, when Jake nudged him.

"Dude, you good?"

Liam hesitated. He could lie. Say everything was fine.

Or...

He sighed. *"I don't know, man. My body feels weird. Nothing fits, and it's like I don't even look like me anymore."*

Jake nodded slowly, like he understood.

"Yeah," he said after a moment. *"Been there."*

Liam blinked. *"Wait. What?"*

Jake—who had everything together—had felt this way too?

Jake leaned back. *"When I was your age, I felt like my body was working against me. Some guys were getting taller overnight, some were growing muscle super fast, and I felt stuck. I hated it."*

Liam frowned. *"So what'd you do?"*

Jake smirked. *"I stopped fighting it."*

Liam stared. *"What does that even mean?"*

Jake pulled something out of his pocket—a worn leather wristband.

"My dad gave me this when I was going through it," he said, handing it to Liam. *"He told me that every awkward stage I went through— every time I felt uncomfortable—was just part of becoming who I was meant to be."*

Liam ran his fingers over the wristband. The leather was smooth, broken in. It felt like it had been through a lot.

Jake clapped a hand on Liam's shoulder. *"Look, man. Your body isn't against you. It's just growing in its own way. Give it time."*

He hesitated for a second, then slid the wristband onto Liam's wrist.

"Keep it," Jake said. *"It's a reminder. You don't have to rush it. Just take things one step at a time."* Liam swallowed hard. The wristband felt solid. Like an anchor.

Maybe, just maybe, this wasn't the end of the world.

By the time Saturday arrived, Liam still wasn't thrilled about shopping. Liam sat in the passenger seat of the car, arms crossed as his mom pulled into the parking lot of the clothing store.

He still didn't want to be here.

The thought of stepping into the dressing room, standing in front of a mirror under those bright, unforgiving lights made his stomach twist.

But then his fingers brushed against the leather wristband Jake had given him. He stared down at it, turning it over between his fingers.

"You don't have to rush it. Just take things one step at a time." Jake's words stuck with him.

Liam took a deep breath and stepped out of the car.

Maybe he wasn't ready. But at least he was here.

The store was packed with racks of jeans, hoodies, and sneakers.

His mom grabbed a few options and handed them to him. *"Just try them on,"* she said gently. *"See what fits."*

Liam hesitated outside the dressing room, staring at the curtain. The weight of expectation hung over him. Then he looked down at his wristband again.

"One step at a time." Liam pushed the curtain aside and stepped in.

The mirror loomed in front of him as he pulled on a new shirt.

It fit better than his old one, but it still felt... weird. Different.

His shoulders looked broader than before. His arms had more definition. But instead of feeling stronger, he just felt out of place. He turned to the side, tugging at the fabric.

Then, for the first time in a long while, he didn't immediately look away.

He let himself really see the reflection. Not perfect. Not terrible. Just... him.

Liam stepped out of the dressing room.

His mom looked up, smiling. *"How do they feel?"*

Liam shrugged, shifting in the new clothes.

"It's... okay." And surprisingly, he meant it.

For the first time in weeks, he wasn't trying to hide.

He wasn't overthinking it. It wasn't perfect, and he still had a long way to go. But he had crossed the first threshold. And that was something.

Monday morning, Liam walked into school in his new clothes. They fit well. They felt comfortable. But as soon as he stepped into the crowded hallway, the doubt came creeping back.

Some of the guys in his class seemed taller overnight. Some were already hitting the gym, getting ripped fast.

Others still looked like kids. And Liam felt stuck somewhere in the middle.

Not big enough. Not small enough. Not enough.

At lunch, his friend Josh sat across from him, shoveling fries into his mouth.

Josh was on the basketball team, tall and lean. He had never seemed to stress about this stuff.

"I've been hitting the gym with my brother," Josh said between bites. *"You should come. Might help, you know... build some muscle."*

Liam froze.

"Might help."

He knew Josh wasn't trying to insult him.

But suddenly, Liam felt like Josh saw him as weak.

Like he needed to fix something. The words sat heavy in his chest. Maybe Josh was right. Maybe he wasn't enough as he was.

Josh's words stuck with him.

That night, Liam stood in front of his bedroom mirror again.

This time, he didn't see the progress. Didn't see the small steps he had taken. All he saw were the ways he didn't measure up.

He rolled the wristband between his fingers. Earlier, it had felt like an anchor. Now, it felt like a reminder of how far he still had to go.

He took it off and set it on his desk. *"I'm not sure I can do this."*

The reflection staring back at him looked unsure. Trapped between who he was and who he was supposed to be. And for the first time, he wasn't sure which one was real.

Liam sat on the edge of his bed, staring at the wristband Jake had given him. It had been a comfort at first. A reminder that he wasn't alone. But right now, it didn't feel like enough.

In the dim light of his room, he slowly unfastened it and set it on his nightstand.

"I'm not sure I can do this."

The reflection in the dark window stared back at him, uncertain.

Was he supposed to keep pushing forward? Or had he already lost?

Just as Liam sank back onto his bed, his phone buzzed. He hesitated before picking it up.

It was a text from Jake: *"Remember, your body is your journey. No one else's."*

Liam blinked. How did Jake always know the right thing to say? The words lingered in his mind.

Maybe he wasn't failing. Maybe this was just part of figuring things out. But how long was it going to take?

The next day at school, a new challenge arrived. Josh and the guys were talking about a pool party that weekend.

Liam was halfway to his locker when he overheard them. *"Yeah, I got some new swim trunks,"* one of the guys said. *"Been hitting the gym hard—gotta be ready, you know?"*

The others laughed, flexing their arms.

Liam froze. He didn't have abs. He didn't even feel comfortable in his own skin.

The thought of standing shirtless around all those guys—showing his awkward, half-grown body—made him feel sick.

That night, Liam sat by his window, staring at the sky. The moon hung low, casting shadows across his room.

His mind kept replaying their words. *"Been hitting the gym hard—gotta be ready."*

He looked down at his arms. They weren't weak, but they weren't impressive either. He exhaled sharply.

"I can't do it. I don't belong at that party."

But then, a small voice pushed back. *"You've come this far. Why turn back now?"*

Liam's jaw tightened. Why was he letting this fear control him?

Why was he acting like he had something to prove?

For the first time in weeks, he let go of the idea of being perfect. Instead, he asked himself a different question:

"Do I really want to keep hiding?"

The reflection in his window wasn't clear. But for the first time, he didn't hate it.

The day of the pool party arrived. Liam stood in front of his mirror, heart racing. He wasn't confident. But he wasn't running either.

He grabbed his favorite swim trunks—nothing flashy, just something that felt right.

It was the first real choice he had made about his body that wasn't driven by fear.

Not hiding. Not proving anything. Just being himself.

As Liam walked into the backyard, he could feel eyes on him. His stomach clenched.

The pool shimmered under the summer sun, kids laughing and diving in.

Josh spotted him and waved. *"Dude, you made it!"*

Liam nodded, exhaling slowly.

He pulled off his shirt, feeling the heat of the sun—and his own nerves—on his skin.

But this time, he didn't flinch. No one was staring. No one was judging him. He had built up this fear in his head for so long... and for what?

Josh grinned, tossing a ball at him. *"Let's go! You're on my team."*

Liam caught it, grinning back. And just like that...

He was in the water, laughing, playing, living. Liam hadn't magically become confident.

He hadn't fixed everything. But he had faced one of his biggest fears. And the world hadn't ended.

He had shown up—just as he was.

And that was enough.

As the afternoon sun faded after the pool party, Liam sat on his bed, thinking. Maybe this is what Jake meant. It's not about changing everything. It's about showing up—giving myself the chance to be okay with who I am, step by step.

It had only been a week since the party, but something inside him had shifted.

Standing in front of his mirror, he expected to feel the usual frustration—the instinct to criticize everything he saw.

But today? It wasn't quite as loud.

The mirror, which once felt like a judge, now felt more like a neutral observer.

It wasn't telling him he wasn't good enough. It was just showing him where he was.

And maybe, for the first time, that was okay.

Liam grabbed his sketchbook—the same one he had ignored for weeks.

He paused, glancing at his reflection one last time. *"I'm not completely there yet... but maybe that's okay."*

His conversation with Jake echoed in his mind.

"You're evolving, Liam. And that's what matters."

For the first time, he felt like he was starting to believe it.

The next morning at school, the usual nerves were still there. But something else was there too. A new kind of energy.

As Liam walked through the hallways, he could feel the same stares from classmates.

Some of them had already bulked up—taller, stronger, more defined. Some still looked like their younger selves. And then there was him—stuck somewhere in between.

Before, he would've shrunk under their eyes. But today, he didn't.

He held his head high, not because he thought he had changed overnight, but because he didn't feel like hiding anymore.

And that? That was progress.

As Liam walked into class, his best friend, Jordan, jogged up beside him.

"You good for the presentation later?" Jordan asked, glancing at him. Liam hesitated for a moment. Then he nodded. *"Yeah, actually, I am."*

And he was surprised to find... he meant it.

Their assignment was to present something personal—something meaningful.

For Liam, the choice was clear. His sketches.

The ones he had drawn when he felt awkward, lost, frustrated with himself. The ones that captured his body changing in ways he didn't understand. The ones that made him feel seen, even when he didn't like what he saw.

This was his story. And for the first time, he was ready to share it.

As Liam stood in front of the class, the old self-consciousness crept in. For a split second, he considered playing it safe. But then he took a breath.

And instead of hiding, he flipped open his sketchbook.

Liam stood at the front of the classroom, his fingers resting on the edges of his sketchbook. His heart pounded in his chest, but he wasn't running from it this time.

He glanced at his classmates—some watching with curiosity, others barely paying attention. But this moment wasn't for them.

It was for him. Taking a deep breath, Liam began.

"I've spent a lot of time feeling awkward about myself."

His voice wasn't loud, but it was steady.

"I kept comparing myself to everyone else, wondering why I wasn't growing like them—or why I was changing in ways that made me feel uncomfortable."

He flipped open his sketchbook, revealing a series of drawings—each one a snapshot of the different stages he had been through.

Some pages showed his arms too thin, his shoulders narrow.

Others captured the moments when he felt too big, too clumsy, too out of place in his own skin.

"But I'm starting to realize something," Liam continued, his gaze moving across the room. *"These changes? They're not something to fight. They're just part of growing up. We all go through them differently, and that's okay."*

The class was silent.

But for the first time in a long while, Liam didn't mistake that silence for judgment.

It wasn't fear or embarrassment holding him back anymore. It was pride.

After school, Liam walked home, the warm afternoon sun on his back.

There was a lightness in his step—not because anything had magically changed, but because he had stopped carrying the weight of trying to be someone else.

His body hadn't suddenly looked the way he once wished it would.

His height, his build, the way his features were still shifting—all of it was still there. But the shame wasn't.

Because for the first time, he wasn't letting it control him.

As Liam reached his front porch, he paused. He pulled out his sketchbook and flipped to a blank page.

His fingers traced the empty space, thinking about everything he had been through. This was his story. And he was in control of how it unfolded.

At that moment, Liam realized he had found his elixir. Not in the form of bigger muscles or perfect proportions. But in the knowledge that his body was just one part of him.

It didn't define his worth.

He was strong, creative, and evolving. Sure, he had insecurities. But he also had something bigger: resilience.

He picked up his pencil, letting new lines take shape on the page. *"This is me,"* Liam thought, a small smile forming. *"And I'm finally okay with that."*

Learning Lessons from "This Is Me"

Your body is a story of growth, change, and resilience.

Liam's journey shows that it's okay to feel unsure as you navigate the changes in how you look and feel. What matters most is finding the courage to accept those changes and remember that your worth is so much more than how you appear.

It's easy to compare yourself to others—to the guys in your class, to athletes, to what you see online. But like Liam realized, everyone's journey is different. There's no single "right" way to grow, and what makes you unique is what makes you strong.

Sometimes, the hardest part of self-acceptance is facing what scares you. Whether it's speaking up, stepping out of your comfort zone, or showing up as your true self, those choices build confidence—one step at a time.

And remember: you're not alone. Liam had Jake, just like you have people who care about you. Honest conversations with friends, family, or mentors can remind you that you don't have to figure everything out by yourself.

Most importantly, self-acceptance isn't an overnight thing. It's a process. Each time you choose to own your journey, you get one step closer to seeing that you were enough all along.

Story 6 - True to Me

The morning sun cast long shadows over the boardwalk as Leo, fourteen and restless, wiped down the counter of his family's seaside diner. The familiar scent of bacon and freshly brewed coffee filled the air, blending with the salty breeze rolling in from the ocean. Tourists wandered past the windows, scanning the menu, while a few regulars sat at the counter sipping their morning coffee.

Leo usually found comfort in the rhythm of the diner—the clatter of plates, the hum of conversation, the steady crash of waves outside—but today, his chest felt tight, as if something heavy had settled inside him.

From behind, his mom's voice drifted over. *"Hey, bud, you should think about skipping the pancakes today. A protein shake might be a better way to start the morning."*

Leo's hand paused over the plate of stacked pancakes he had just set down for himself. He glanced up, catching his reflection in the diner's steel napkin dispenser—just for a second—but long enough to notice how his t-shirt stretched tighter across his shoulders than it used to.

His older brother, Sam, sat at the counter scrolling through his phone, barely looking up as he added, *"Yeah, man, Coach says it's all about clean eating and getting strong. Maybe you should start lifting with me. It'd help you feel more confident."*

Leo forced a small nod and muttered, *"Yeah... maybe."* But deep inside, his stomach twisted.

Sam was the guy everyone liked—captain of the soccer team, confident, athletic. Their mom always talked about how "dedicated" and "disciplined" he was. And Leo? Leo liked sketching. He liked designing characters, worlds, stories. He wasn't scrawny, but he wasn't ripped like Sam either. And every time someone mentioned what he should eat, how he should train, or how he should "carry himself more confidently", it felt like a reminder that he wasn't measuring up.

Later that afternoon, Leo leaned against the counter, staring out the diner's big windows. The lunch rush had slowed, leaving only the hum of the radio and the occasional clang of dishes from the back. Sam and their mom sat at a booth, talking in low voices about Sam's new workout routine.

Then, his mom glanced over. *"Leo, you should start coming to the gym with us. It could be a good bonding thing—getting strong together as a family."*

Leo hesitated. He could feel Sam watching him, expectant.

They meant well. They weren't saying he wasn't good enough—not directly. But the message was there, sitting beneath their words like a weight pressing down on his chest.

He wanted to say no. He wanted to tell them that lifting weights and counting protein grams wasn't him. But part of him also wondered... Would they respect him more if he just tried? Would he feel more comfortable in his own skin?

"...Yeah, I'll think about it," he mumbled.

His mom smiled, satisfied. Sam gave him a small nod of approval. But Leo's stomach churned as he turned back to wiping the counter.

That evening, Leo sat in his room, sketchbook open but untouched.

The lamp on his desk flickered softly, casting shadows over his collection of drawings—characters he'd designed, superheroes, warriors, people with confidence he wished he had. He ran a hand through his messy brown hair and exhaled.

Then, he glanced at his reflection in the window.

"Why can't I just be okay with how I am?"

He wasn't out of shape, but he wasn't built like Sam. He wasn't unathletic, but he wasn't one of the guys on the team either.

What was wrong with just being him?

The next day, Leo worked the afternoon shift, taking orders and refilling ketchup bottles when the bell over the diner door jingled. Ray, a middle-aged tattoo artist from the shop next door, strolled in, setting his sunglasses on the counter.

Ray was the kind of guy who always seemed comfortable in his own skin—broad-shouldered, covered in ink, and never in a hurry.

"Yo, kid," Ray said, leaning against the counter. *"You look like someone stole your fries. What's up?"*

Leo sighed, debating whether to brush it off. But Ray wasn't the kind of guy you had to pretend with.

"It's just... I feel like I don't fit what people expect me to be," Leo admitted. *"Like, I should be stronger, more confident. I don't know. It's dumb."*

Ray raised an eyebrow. *"Dumb? Sounds like a real thing to me."*

He reached into his bag and pulled out a small, worn sketchbook with rough designs and faded ink sketches. He slid it across the counter.

"When I was your age, I was caught up in trying to be what people wanted, too. I thought being tough meant I had to act a certain way. Took me years to figure out that my strength wasn't in being the biggest guy in the room—it was in what I could create."

Leo flipped through the pages. The designs were raw but detailed—unfinished tattoos, character sketches, ideas that hadn't fully formed.

"You want to know the best part?" Ray asked. *"No one else gets to decide what goes in here except you."*

Leo's fingers tightened around the book. Something about it—about having a space that was his, a place where he could create without judgment—sent a quiet spark through his chest.

"Thanks," he said, his voice a little steadier.

Ray smirked. *"Anytime, kid. Just remember—you don't have to prove anything to anyone. You just gotta figure out who you are and own it."*

Leo nodded, feeling—for the first time in a while—like maybe that was possible.

That night, Leo sat at his desk, sketchbook open but untouched. A half-drawn superhero stared back at him—broad-shouldered, confident, completely sure of himself. Everything Leo didn't feel.

He picked up his pencil, hesitating. Then, instead of finishing the superhero, he let his hand move freely—not drawing muscles or masks, just lines, shapes, a blur of frustration spilling onto the page.

His mom's voice echoed in his mind. *"Protein shakes are better for you."*

Sam's words followed. *"It'll help you feel more confident."*

Leo pressed the pencil harder against the page.

After a while, he found himself sketching a figure standing on a rooftop, looking out over a vast city, the wind pushing against him. The figure wasn't flexing, wasn't standing like a champion. He was just... there. Holding his ground. Unmoved by the world's expectations.

Leo exhaled. Maybe he wasn't ready to say how he felt out loud, but at least here, in his sketchbook, he could be honest.

This was his first step—a small but powerful act of owning his voice.

As summer rolled in, the diner buzzed with customers, tourists piling in for breakfast plates and burgers, the air thick with the smell of coffee and frying bacon.

Leo worked the counter, taking orders and refilling baskets of fries, but his mind kept drifting back to something his mom had said earlier that morning.

"Maybe wear a button-down today, Leo. We want to look sharp for the customers."

Sam had backed her up. *"Yeah, man, it's all about the first impression."*

Leo had nodded, thrown on a flannel over his usual t-shirt, but the words stuck with him.

What was wrong with how he already looked?

He glanced down at the tattoo design book Ray had given him, hidden under the counter. He wanted to flip through it, let himself get lost in the sketches—but Sam's voice lingered in his head.

"You need to start thinking about the image you put out there."

Just then, Sam strolled into the diner with a few friends from soccer practice, still in their training gear, laughing as they took a booth near the window. One of them gave Leo a nod.

"You should come train with us, man," Sam said, drumming his fingers on the table. *"You'd bulk up fast."*

Leo forced a grin. *"Maybe."*

Sam clapped him on the shoulder, not unkindly, but like he was trying to push Leo into place—like an older brother should.

Leo turned away before they could see his expression.

He didn't want to train with them. He didn't want to force himself into their version of what confidence looked like.

But every time he pushed back, it felt like he was letting them down.

Later that afternoon, as Leo wiped down tables near the window, the bell over the diner door jingled.

Ray walked in. Tattooed arms, sunglasses perched on his head, the same easy-going presence as always.

"Yo, kid," he greeted, sliding into a seat. *"You look like you're losing a battle with your own thoughts."*

Leo gave a short laugh, but it wasn't a real one. He hesitated, then said, *"It's just... everyone seems to have an opinion on who I should be. How I should act. How I should look."*

Ray raised an eyebrow. *"Yeah? And what do you think?"*

Leo frowned, arms crossed over his chest. *"I don't know anymore."*

Ray leaned forward, resting his arms on the counter. *"Listen, kid. The mirror? It only shows one part of you. It doesn't show your ideas. It doesn't show what you can make. It doesn't show what actually makes you, you."*

Leo blinked. The words settled deep.

Ray tapped the counter lightly. *"People are always gonna have expectations. You just gotta decide which ones are worth listening to."*

Leo nodded slowly. For the first time all day, the weight in his chest lifted—just a little.

Maybe he wasn't ready to push back yet. But he didn't have to let their expectations define him either.

A few days later, on a quiet night, Leo sat hunched over his desk, the sketchbook Ray had given him open in front of him. He wasn't drawing superheroes this time. He wasn't even sketching designs. Just lines— jagged, rushed, uncertain.

His pencil moved in sharp, frustrated strokes, the page filling with shapes that didn't make sense, like he was trying to put something into words that he didn't know how to say.

Then, without thinking, he drew a figure standing on a rooftop, looking out over the city. It wasn't the strong, muscle-bound hero he used to draw. This one was smaller, standing with his hands in his pockets, shoulders tense.

Leo stared at it. That's me.

Torn between who he wanted to be and who everyone else expected him to become.

He clenched his jaw. Why do I even care so much? Why can't I just ignore it?

But he already knew the answer. Because it was his family. And because Sam wasn't just some guy at school—he was his older brother. The one who always seemed to have it together. The one their mom listened to.

Leo wanted their approval. He wanted to be someone they were proud of. But at what cost?

Could he really keep forcing himself to be something he wasn't?

The next day, Leo's mom suggested a family outing—a late-night drive to the coast. Sam was home from training for the weekend, and she thought it would be a nice way to spend time together.

Leo wasn't sure how he felt about it, but he went along anyway. Maybe the fresh air would clear his head.

The drive was quiet, the only sounds coming from the radio and the steady hum of the car. Leo stared out the window, watching as the city lights faded into the open stretch of highway.

When they reached the beach, they walked along the boardwalk, the sound of waves crashing softly against the shore.

It should have been peaceful.

But Leo felt the weight of unspoken words pressing down on him, heavier than the ocean air.

Then, as if she could sense it, his mom finally spoke.

"You know, Leo, if you wanted, you and Sam could start going to the gym together. It might be fun. A good way to push yourself a little."

Leo stopped walking.

His hands clenched into fists. He knew his mom wasn't trying to be harsh, but it felt like she was confirming what he had feared all along.

That he wasn't enough as he was.

He took a deep breath and turned to her. *"Mom... can we just hang out without talking about how I need to change?"*

She blinked, surprised by the frustration in his voice. *"Leo, that's not what I meant. I just want you to feel good about yourself."*

"I know," Leo said, trying to keep his voice steady. *"But when you and Sam keep talking about working out and getting stronger, it makes me feel like I'm not good enough already."*

The words felt impossible to say—but as soon as they were out, a strange sense of relief followed.

His mom looked at him for a long moment. She didn't brush it off. She didn't argue. Instead, she nodded slowly, something shifting in her expression.

"I didn't realize it felt that way to you," she said softly.

Beside her, Sam didn't say anything at first, just looked out at the water.

Then, after a moment, he shrugged. *"You don't have to do any of that if you don't want to, man. I just thought it'd be good for you."*

Leo let out a breath he hadn't realized he'd been holding. For the first time, it felt like they were actually listening.

That night, when Leo got home, he opened his sketchbook again.

He flipped past the jagged lines, past the first rooftop drawing, to a fresh page.

And this time, when he sketched the figure, the lines were different.

Stronger. More defined.

Still standing on the rooftop, but this time, his shoulders weren't tense. His hands weren't in his pockets. He wasn't trying to be anything. He was just standing there, looking out over the city. Solid. Certain. Himself.

Leo set his pencil down and stared at the drawing. For the first time, it actually felt like him.

Before he went to bed, he whispered to himself, *"I don't have to change for anyone. I can just be... me."*

And this time, it felt real.

The next morning, Sam was restocking supplies at the diner counter when Leo walked in.

"Hey," Sam said, glancing up. *"Gonna hit the gym later. You sure you don't wanna join?"*

Leo hesitated. This was the moment where he usually felt like he had to say yes. But he didn't.

Instead, he took a deep breath and said, *"Thanks, but I think I'm good. Maybe I'll teach you some drawing instead."*

Sam raised an eyebrow, but then, to Leo's surprise, he smirked.

"Yeah? Alright. I'd like that."

Leo smiled. For the first time, it felt like they were meeting in the middle.

That night, Leo's family sat down for dinner, the usual spread of home-cooked dishes on the table. His mom started talking about portion sizes and healthy habits, just like always.

Normally, Leo would stay quiet, eat carefully, and try not to get pulled into the conversation.

But tonight was different. He put his fork down, took a steadying breath, and spoke up.

"Mom, Sam... I know you both just want the best for me. And I appreciate that." He looked between them, pushing past the nervous knot in his stomach. *"But when there are so many comments about what I should be doing differently, it's hard for me to feel good about myself."*

His mom and Sam both looked up. Sam actually stopped chewing.

Leo's voice grew steadier. *"I want to be healthy. But I also want to figure out what that means for me, not just do what works for you guys."*

The room fell quiet for a moment. Then, his mom nodded slowly, a new softness in her expression.

"I didn't realize it felt that way to you," she admitted.

Sam leaned back in his chair, thinking. After a beat, he gave a short nod. *"I get that. You gotta do your thing."*

Leo let out a breath he hadn't realized he was holding. They weren't fighting him. They were listening.

The next morning, Leo walked down to the docks with his sketchbook under his arm. He found his usual spot—a quiet bench where he could watch the fishing boats come and go.

He flipped open his sketchbook, fingers tracing over the latest drawing he'd started. It was the figure from before—the one on the rooftop.

Only now, the lines were clearer. The figure wasn't standing in the shadows anymore, uncertain.

He stood with confidence. Hands in his pockets, staring straight ahead, no longer looking for approval.

Leo grabbed his pencil and added the final details. This wasn't about proving himself to his family anymore.

It was about being okay with who he was.

He wasn't Sam. He wasn't a future athlete or someone who needed to change to fit in. He was himself. And for the first time, that felt like enough.

As he closed the sketchbook and looked out over the water, he felt it - a sense of certainty settling deep inside him.

No matter what came next, he knew one thing for sure: He wasn't changing for anyone but himself.

Learning Lessons from "True to Me"

Leo's journey reminds you that your worth isn't tied to meeting others' expectations. It's easy to feel pressure—from family, friends, or even yourself—to be a certain way, look a certain way, or fit into a mold that doesn't feel right. But the truth is, who you are is already enough.

Leo realized that being strong doesn't mean fitting into someone else's version of success. Strength can mean standing up for yourself, speaking your truth, or simply choosing to accept who you are instead of changing to please others.

Leo learned that if something doesn't feel right, it's okay to say so. Setting boundaries—like telling his family that their constant advice felt like pressure—helped them understand his perspective. The people who truly care about you will listen when you speak up.

Just like Leo, you have the right to define who you are. You don't need permission to be yourself, and you don't have to fit anyone else's mold to be valuable. True confidence comes from embracing your individuality, standing by your choices, and knowing that you are already enough.

Story 7 - Beyond the Game

From the moment Mauricio first picked up a basketball ball, he knew it was more than just a game—it was his game. He spent nearly every afternoon at the neighborhood court, practicing his jump shots, weaving through imaginary defenders, and pushing himself to improve. Basketball wasn't just something he did—it was who he was.

But this year felt different. Tryouts for the school team were coming up, and while Mauricio had always dreamed of playing for the team, a strange mix of excitement and doubt settled in his chest.

"This is the year," he told himself. *"I'm going to make it."*

Yet, in the back of his mind, a smaller, quieter voice whispered something else.

Mauricio had overheard some of the guys talking in the locker room last season.

"Mauricio's got skills, but he doesn't really look like a serious player."

"Yeah, man, it's not just about playing good—it's about having that presence, you know?"

The words stuck to him like a shadow, resurfacing every time he stepped onto the court.

Even now, standing at the free-throw line, he couldn't shake them.

Mauricio bounced the basketball ball rhythmically, staring at the hoop. The steady scuff of the ball against the pavement, the smell of the sun-warmed court, the familiar weight of the ball in his hands—this was where he felt at home.

Across the court, a group of younger kids were playing, laughing, and hyping each other up. They didn't care how they looked or who was watching. They just played because they loved it.

Mauricio inhaled deeply, rolling the ball between his fingers.

"This is where I feel like myself."

No expectations. No judgments. Just the game. Just him.

A few days later, tryouts finally arrived.

Mauricio stood outside the gym doors, his heart pounding.

He'd put in countless hours of practice all summer, working on his speed, his defense, his shooting form.

"I'm ready," he told himself.

As the coach called out names for warm-ups, Mauricio adjusted his jersey, focusing on the sound of sneakers squeaking on the polished floor. But just as he was about to step forward, he heard them.

A couple of players were talking near the bleachers. Their voices were low, but the words cut through the noise like a knife.

"Mauricio's got some talent, but... I don't know, man."

"Coach wants players who look the part, not just play it."

Mauricio's grip tightened around his jersey. The same doubt he thought he had pushed away came rushing back.

"Maybe they have a point."

"I love basketball... but maybe I don't fit what they're looking for."

That night, Mauricio lay in bed, staring at the ceiling, replaying the conversation over and over.

The excitement of tryouts was gone, replaced by a heavy feeling in his chest.

The next afternoon, Mauricio walked past the neighborhood court—the same court where he had spent so many hours perfecting his game.

Normally, he would have sprinted onto the pavement, feeling the ball in his hands before his backpack even hit the ground.

But today, he hesitated.

For the first time, the court felt different.

The hoop seemed higher, the court longer, the game further away.

Instead of stepping in, he turned away.

"What's the point of trying if they don't think I belong?"

His hands tightened around the straps of his backpack as he walked away.

"Maybe they're right... maybe I just don't have the right look for it."

A storm of doubt and frustration swirled inside him.

Was his love for the game enough?

The following weekend, Mauricio found himself at the neighborhood basketball court, alone with nothing but his thoughts and the rhythmic bounce of the ball. Normally, the court was his escape—his place to forget about everything else.

But today, it felt emptier than usual.

He dribbled slowly, his mind clouded by the tryouts and the whispers that still lingered in his head.

"Maybe I don't fit what they're looking for."

He took a shot. The ball bounced off the rim.

"Maybe I never will."

As he grabbed the rebound, a voice called out from the side of the court.

"Nice arc on that shot. You've got a solid follow-through."

Mauricio turned and saw Coach Andrés, an ex-player who ran community leagues and had a reputation for mentoring young athletes. He wasn't just about skill—he cared about mindset.

Mauricio forced a small smile. *"Thanks, Coach."*

Andrés walked onto the court, spinning a ball on his fingertips. *"You know, when I was your age, I let people's opinions mess with my head too. I wanted to be a point guard, but people kept saying I didn't have the 'right build' for it."* He chuckled. *"I almost quit."*

Mauricio looked up, curiosity flickering in his eyes. *"What did you do?"*

Andrés stopped spinning the ball and held it out to Mauricio.

"I stopped letting other people tell me what I could or couldn't be. I realized my real strength wasn't about size or looks—it was about how much I loved the game."

Mauricio caught the ball, gripping it tightly.

Coach Andrés reached into his pocket and pulled out a wristband, tossing it to him. It was engraved with the words:

"Strength Comes from Within."

"Wear this as a reminder," Andrés said. *"The ones who judge you by how you look? They don't see the whole picture. You've got something special, Mauricio. Don't let anyone make you forget that."*

Mauricio stared at the wristband, a strange warmth settling in his chest.

For the first time since tryouts, he felt a flicker of confidence push back against the doubt.

"Maybe Coach Andrés is right."

He clenched his fist, a new resolve forming.

"I love this game more than anything. Isn't that what should matter?"

Later that week, Mauricio walked back into the school gym. The weight of his worries was still there, but Andrés' words echoed in his mind.

Across the gym, a few players were practicing shots, including some of the same teammates who had made him feel like an outsider.

He hesitated for a second, his fingers brushing over the wristband on his wrist.

Then, he tightened his laces and stepped forward.

He grabbed a ball, and a few teammates glanced over, surprised.

But Mauricio didn't care. This wasn't about proving himself to them anymore.

It was about reclaiming the game he loved.

Dribble. Step. Jump shot.

The ball swished cleanly through the net.

Mauricio exhaled, his shoulders relaxing for the first time in days.

"I may not look like what they expect."

"But that doesn't mean I don't belong."

As he turned to leave, he caught one last look at the court.

The doubt was still there—but it wasn't as loud anymore.

Coach Andrés' words stayed with him:

"You've got something special, Mauricio."

And this time, he believed it.

The next morning, Mauricio's alarm went off before sunrise. For a split second, he thought about hitting snooze.

Then, he remembered why he was doing this. He got up, laced his sneakers, and headed to the gym.

When he arrived, the court was completely empty, bathed in soft morning light. He bounced the ball, the sound echoing against the walls.

No crowd. No pressure. Just the game and him.

"I'm doing this for me."

The wristband felt warm against his skin.

"I'm here because I love it."

As he left the gym, a small smile tugged at the corners of his mouth.

Tomorrow, he'd be back.

And this time, nothing was going to stop him.

At school, Mauricio was starting to feel the weight of every glance, every whisper.

During lunch, as he grabbed his tray and walked toward an empty table, he overheard a couple of teammates talking at the next table over.

One of them laughed. *"Yeah, Mauricio's got hustle, but let's be real—he just doesn't look like a real player."*

Another shrugged. *"He works hard, sure, but I don't see him fitting in with the team. It just doesn't look... right."*

Mauricio froze for a second, his grip tightening on his tray.

"Again with this?"

Even after all his early mornings, all his extra hours on the court, it still wasn't enough for them.

His stomach twisted. He wasn't sure if it was frustration or just plain exhaustion.

Without a word, he turned away and sat at a table by himself.

A few moments later, someone set their tray down across from him.

Mauricio looked up—it was Daniel, a kid from his math class. They'd never really talked before.

"Mind if I sit here?" Daniel asked casually.

Mauricio just nodded.

Daniel unwrapped his sandwich and took a bite before speaking again. *"You know, I see you at the gym every morning. Pretty impressive that you're sticking with it."*

Mauricio gave a small, tired smile. *"Thanks... I just wish it felt like enough. Sometimes I don't even know if I'm doing this for me or to prove something."*

Daniel nodded. *"Trust me, I get it. But the thing is—no one else knows how much this means to you but you. That's what makes it worth doing."*

Mauricio let that sink in.

Maybe Daniel had a point.

For the first time in a while, Mauricio felt like someone actually understood what he was going through.

And that felt good.

With Daniel's words lingering in his mind, Mauricio pushed himself even harder.

He stayed longer after school, took more shots, ran more drills.

But no matter how much he worked, the weight of judgment didn't go away.

One evening, during a scrimmage, the coach called him aside. *"Mauricio,"* the coach started, his voice not unkind, but hesitant. *"I see you're putting in a lot of effort... but basketball requires a certain... form."*

Mauricio felt his chest tighten.

"There's a balance," the coach continued. *"A... look. Maybe there's another way you could contribute to the team."*

Mauricio stood there, his mind racing.

He had heard those words before.

Not built for this. Doesn't fit the mold. Doesn't look like a player.

The words echoed in his head like a broken record.

Mauricio nodded numbly and walked away, heading toward the empty bleachers.

His teammates kept playing, running up and down the court, laughing and calling out plays—but it all felt distant.

He gripped his wristband, the one Andrés gave him.

"I've put in everything I have... but what if it's still not enough?"

He stared at the court, once his favorite place in the world. Now, it just felt like a reminder of what he wasn't.

The next day, Mauricio skipped practice. He couldn't bring himself to go back. Instead, he wandered through town until he ended up at the community center.

Andrés was there, painting a mural along the outer wall, a massive piece filled with vibrant blues and golds.

He didn't say anything at first—he just handed Mauricio a paintbrush.

Mauricio hesitated before taking it. Andrés gave him a knowing look. *"Had a feeling you'd come by. Something's on your mind, isn't it?"*

Mauricio sighed, swirling the paint in slow strokes. *"They don't think I have the right look. They say I'm not 'built' for basketball. I don't know why I'm even trying anymore."*

Andrés dipped his brush into a new color and kept painting.

After a moment, he spoke.

"Mauricio... if you love something, you don't need anyone's permission to keep doing it."

Mauricio glanced at him, unsure.

Andrés smiled. *"This isn't about how they see you. It's about how you see yourself. You don't fit a mold because you're creating your own path."*

Mauricio stared at the mural, the swirls of color blending together into something unexpected, different—powerful.

And for the first time in days, he didn't feel as lost.

Andrés dipped his brush into a deep shade of blue, adding bold strokes to the mural. The image of a lone figure, standing tall against a storm, was slowly coming to life.

Mauricio watched for a moment before picking up a brush himself. Something about the painting felt familiar—like it was telling his own story.

He hesitated before pressing the brush against the wall.

Andrés glanced over at him. *"You know, you don't need permission to do what you love, Mauricio."*

Mauricio looked up.

"This isn't about how they see you," Andrés continued, his voice steady. *"It's about how you see yourself. You don't fit a mold because you're creating your own path."*

Andrés' words settled over Mauricio like a switch flipping inside him.

For the first time, he saw it clearly.

His worth wasn't tied to whether his teammates thought he belonged. It wasn't about their approval. It wasn't about the coach's doubts.

It was about his love for the game.

Mauricio pressed the brush against the mural, adding streaks of fiery orange behind the figure in the storm. The frustration, the doubt, the pressure—it all flowed into each brushstroke.

And slowly, those feelings began to change.

By the time he set the brush down, his hands were covered in paint, but his heart felt lighter than it had in weeks.

The next morning, Mauricio woke up before his alarm.

He laced up his sneakers, grabbed his basketball, and headed straight to the gym.

Not to prove anything. Not to fit anyone's idea of what a player should be.

But to take back the game that he loved.

He arrived early, before anyone else, the empty gym bathed in the golden morning light.

Mauricio took a deep breath and stepped onto the court. The sound of the ball bouncing against the floor, the soft squeak of his sneakers—it all felt right again.

By the time the other players arrived, he was already drenched in sweat, pushing himself harder than ever.

His movements were sharper, his confidence stronger. The hesitation was gone.

And people started to notice.

During practice, Mauricio's intensity surprised his teammates. He was faster, more focused, and sharper than before.

Even the coach took notice.

By the end of the session, Mauricio stood by the baseline, catching his breath, when Coach walked over.

"Mauricio," he said, arms crossed. Mauricio wiped sweat from his forehead, bracing himself for whatever was coming next.

"I've seen a lot of players come and go," the coach continued, his voice unreadable. *"But not many come back stronger after being knocked down."*

Mauricio met his gaze.

The coach nodded. *"You've been putting in the work. You've shown more resilience than most. We're playing a scrimmage against another school team next week. I want to see what you can do."*

Mauricio's breath caught. He had worked for this moment. He earned this moment.

"You mean... you want me to play?" he asked.

Coach gave a small nod. *"Let's see what you've got."*

A rush of excitement surged through Mauricio's chest.

A few weeks ago, he wasn't sure if he'd ever belong here.

Now?

He was going to step onto that court as the player he always knew he was.

The game day arrived. The gym was alive with the sounds of sneakers squeaking against the floor, the echo of bouncing basketballs, and the energy of the crowd.

Mauricio stood near the bench, dressed in his team's colors, the buzz of excitement and nerves pulsing through him.

A few weeks ago, he would have worried about whether people thought he belonged.

But now?

He knew he did.

The whistle blew, signaling the start of the game.

Mauricio took a deep breath, stepping onto the court. He wasn't here to fit someone else's image. He wasn't here to prove anything to anyone. He was here because he loved the game. And that was enough.

The gym buzzed with energy—sneakers squeaking, coaches barking instructions, the crowd murmuring with anticipation. Mauricio took a deep breath, standing at the edge of the court, his heart pounding in time with the bounce of the basketball.

This was it. His chance to play, to show up for himself and no one else.

As the game started, his nerves melted away, replaced by pure instinct. He moved fluidly—passing, cutting, reading the court like it was second nature. This was where he belonged.

During a timeout, he overheard two players from the opposing team talking on the sideline.

"That's him?" one of them muttered. *"He doesn't look like the usual type of player."*

The other shrugged. *"Well, he's out here, isn't he? Guess that means something."*

Mauricio clenched his jaw, but instead of doubt, a fire ignited inside him.

"Let them talk," he thought, his eyes locking onto the hoop. *"I'm not here to impress them. I'm here because I love this game."*

The game was neck and neck in the final seconds. His team was down by one.

Mauricio caught the ball at the three-point line. Everything slowed.

His teammates were calling out. Defenders closed in.

He had a choice—pass or take the shot.

But he already knew the answer.

With one smooth motion, he rose into the air, his form automatic, his confidence unwavering. The ball soared through the air. The buzzer sounded.

Swish.

The gym exploded in cheers. His teammates tackled him in excitement.

But as they shouted his name, the real victory wasn't in their voices. It was in his own.

"I did this. Not for them. For me."

As the celebration settled, Coach walked over.

"Mauricio," he said. Mauricio stood up straighter, bracing himself.

The coach extended a hand. *"You showed real heart out there. I underestimated you—and I'm glad you proved me wrong."*

Mauricio shook his hand, feeling a quiet pride settle in his chest. He appreciated the words, but he no longer needed them.

He wasn't playing for approval anymore. He was playing because he loved it.

That night, Mauricio sat on his bed, a notebook open in front of him.

He scribbled down his thoughts, capturing the journey that had led him here.

"I used to think I had to look a certain way to belong on the court. But I get it now—passion and persistence matter more than any stereotype. I don't have to change to fit anyone's expectations. I just have to stay true to myself."

He thought about Coach. Andrés. Mateo. Each had played a role in his journey, but the final step?

That was his.

The next morning, he jogged to the community court, where a few younger boys were watching from the sidelines.

He smiled and tossed one of them the ball.

"You know," he said, nodding toward the hoop, *"you don't have to look any particular way to love this game. The only thing that matters is that you love it."*

As he watched them start to play, he felt it—a deep satisfaction that had nothing to do with winning or proving himself.

Mauricio had found his strength.

Not through changing himself, but through honoring who he was all along.

Learning Lessons from "Beyond the Game"

Mauricio's story proves that your passion and hard work are more important than fitting into someone else's idea of success.

There will always be people who doubt you, but real confidence isn't about proving them wrong—it's about proving yourself right. Even when Mauricio faced rejection, he showed up. Again and again. That's what made the difference.

Success isn't about fitting a mold—it's about owning your journey. Like Mauricio, you have the power to rise above doubt and follow what you love.

Story 8 - Roots of Confidence

Michael's room was a blend of his worlds—a soccer jersey from his dad's home country draped over his chair, posters of his favorite players on the wall, and a shelf lined with souvenirs his family had brought back from trips to visit relatives.

This was where he felt most like himself, surrounded by reminders of his heritage. His grandfather often shared stories of strength and resilience, tales of their family's history that had always made Michael feel proud of who he was.

But recently, things had changed. High school felt different. It was like there were unspoken rules about how to dress, how to act, even how to look. Michael felt stuck between the warmth of his cultural roots and the pressure to fit in with the guys at school. For the first time, he wasn't sure if he belonged in either place.

Michael sat on the edge of his bed, tying the laces of his worn-out soccer cleats. His grandfather had given them to him, saying they were just like the ones he used to play in as a kid. Normally, wearing them made Michael feel connected to his family's past, but today, he hesitated.

At school, most of the guys wore flashy new sneakers—limited-edition brands, all spotless and expensive. His old cleats suddenly felt out of place.

He grabbed his phone and scrolled through his social media feed. Post after post showed guys at school posing with the latest sneakers, designer hoodies, and slick haircuts. It was the same online as it was in the hallways—an unspoken standard of what was "cool."

"Why don't I fit in like everyone else?" he thought, tapping his cleats against the floor. *"Maybe if I got a new pair, changed my style a little... I wouldn't feel like I'm in two different worlds."*

Michael sighed, tossing his phone onto his bed before heading downstairs. Even as he left for school, the thought stuck with him.

At lunch, Michael sat with his friends in the crowded cafeteria as they talked excitedly about the weekend's big event—a pop-up shop with Ryan Carter, a social media influencer known for his "effortlessly cool" style and massive following. Ryan had become the unofficial role model for most of the guys at school, and everyone wanted to dress like him.

"Can you imagine if we got a picture with him?" Nate said, practically bouncing in his seat.

"Man, I'm gonna try to get those sneakers he wore in his last video," Jason added. *"They drop this weekend, and I need them."*

Turning to Michael, Nate grinned. *"Dude, you should come! It'll be sick. And maybe we can all get a photo with him."*

Michael hesitated, glancing down at his tray. *"I don't know... I'm not really into all that. Besides, I don't exactly have the right look for it."*

Jason and Nate exchanged a quick look—nothing mean, but enough that Michael noticed.

Jason shrugged. *"Your call, man. But it'd be cool to have you there."*

They turned back to their conversation, talking about what outfits they'd wear to match Ryan Carter's style.

Michael stirred his food, the feeling of being on the outside creeping in again. *"Maybe if I dressed more like them, it wouldn't feel like such a big deal,"* he thought.

"But why should I have to change so much?"

The thought sat heavily with him, solidifying the doubt that had been creeping into his mind. He didn't want to feel like an outsider, but he also didn't want to lose the parts of himself that made him who he was.

That evening, Michael stood in front of his bedroom mirror, gripping a pair of brand-new sneakers still in the box. They weren't his usual style—not like the old cleats his grandfather had given him—but they looked just like the ones Ryan Carter wore in his latest post. He set the box down and rubbed the back of his neck, staring at his reflection.

His hair, naturally wavy and thick, had always been a small reminder of his family's heritage. His grandfather used to say, *"Our hair carries history. Don't ever be ashamed of where you come from."* But in the halls of his school, the trend was different—clean, sharp fades, styled just right.

He reached for his phone, scrolling through photos of guys at school. All of them had that same look—the fresh cuts, the sneakers, the confidence. Michael grabbed a comb, flattening his hair, imagining what he'd look like if he cut it short like everyone else.

"Would it really be such a big deal to change? Maybe if I looked more like them, I'd finally feel like I belonged."

His fingers hovered over his hair again, but something inside him hesitated.

"Is this really me?"

The question sat heavy in his chest. His grandfather had always told him to be proud of who he was, but was that pride worth feeling like an outsider?

Michael sighed, ruffling his hair back to the way it naturally fell. He slid the sneakers back into the box and tucked them under his bed. His chest still felt tight, but for some reason, there was also a flicker of relief.

The next day, Michael sat in art class, lost in thought as he absentmindedly doodled patterns in his sketchbook. His teacher, Mr. Alvarez, noticed and walked over, pulling up a chair beside him.

Mr. Alvarez: *"That's some interesting work you've got there, Michael. I've seen you put a lot of heart into your drawings before, but this... this looks like there's more of you in it."*

Michael hesitated, looking down at the swirling patterns and shapes— designs inspired by the artwork his grandfather had hanging in their home. He hadn't even realized he was drawing them.

Michael: *"I dunno... I guess I wasn't really thinking about it."*

Mr. Alvarez: *[nods] "Sometimes, that's when the truest parts of us come out."*

Michael stayed quiet, tapping his pencil against the page.

Michael: *"It's just... I don't know if the real 'me' fits in here. Sometimes, I think it'd be easier to just blend in."*

Mr. Alvarez: *"Fitting in is easy. But the world doesn't need another copy of what's already out there. It needs your voice, your story.*

Maybe instead of trying to disappear into the crowd, try letting your art show who you are. There's strength in that."

Michael let those words settle.

For the first time in days, he felt like maybe his differences weren't something to erase. Maybe they were something valuable.

As he left class, he carried that thought with him.

That night, as Michael got ready for bed, he pulled out his old cleats and ran his fingers over the worn leather. They were scuffed, broken in, but something about them felt... right.

The next morning, he laced them up without hesitation.

Before heading out the door, he caught a glimpse of himself in the hallway mirror. His hair was still thick, still wavy, just like his grandfather's. He had always worn it like this, but today, he made a choice—to wear it not because he hadn't changed it yet, but because he didn't *want* to change it.

"Maybe it's time I stopped hiding."

Walking through the school hallway, Michael felt a mix of pride and nerves. He noticed a few curious glances from classmates, and for a second, his stomach twisted. But instead of shrinking back, he straightened his shoulders.

It was a small step, but it felt big.

For the first time in a long time, he wasn't trying to be someone else. He was walking into school *as himself.*

Michael walked down the hallway, feeling good about his choice—until he caught Ryan and his group glancing at him. Ryan, one of the popular guys at school, smirked as Michael passed.

Ryan: *"Whoa, new look, huh? Didn't know you were trying something... different."*

Michael hesitated. He could hear the mocking edge in Ryan's voice, subtle but sharp.

Michael: *"Yeah, just thought I'd switch things up."*

Ryan shrugged. *"Well, it's... definitely different."* He chuckled, nudging one of his friends.

Michael's stomach tightened. As Ryan walked off, Michael felt the confidence he had earlier slipping away. He could still hear their laughter echoing down the hall.

"Maybe I'm just making things harder for myself. What if they're right? What if I really do stand out... and not in a good way?"

His instinct was to turn around, head to the bathroom, and fix his hair—make it look more like everyone else's. But before he could move, he spotted David, a friend from his soccer team, standing by his locker. David gave him a nod.

David: *"Dude, I like the cleats. They've got character."*

Michael blinked, surprised.

Michael: *"You think so?"*

David: *"Yeah. It's cool when people actually own who they are. Not a lot of guys do."*

Michael felt a small weight lift from his chest. It wasn't much, but having someone in his corner made a difference.

A few days later, Mr. Alvarez assigned an art project for the class.

Mr. Alvarez: *"For this project, I want you all to create self-portraits— not just of how you look, but of who you are. Your identity, your story."*

The class buzzed with excitement, but Michael's hands tightened around his pencil.

As students around him sketched confidently, he hesitated. He wanted to include things that meant something to him—his grandfather's soccer jersey, the patterns from the artwork in their home—but doubt crept in.

"Maybe I should just play it safe. Do something that won't stand out too much. Why does this have to feel so complicated?"

He glanced around. Some of his classmates were already deep into their work, sketching things that fit neatly into the school's unspoken expectations. He felt torn, realizing that if he put his real self into this project, it might draw even more attention.

That evening, Michael sat at the kitchen table, staring at his blank sketchpad. His Abuelito walked in, carrying two mugs of hot chocolate. He set one in front of Michael before sitting down across from him.

Abuelito: *"You look like a man with something heavy on his mind."*

Michael hesitated before sighing.

Michael: *"It's this art project. We're supposed to draw a self-portrait, but... I don't know. I feel like if I put too much of myself into it, it's just going to make me stand out even more. And not in a good way."*

His grandfather nodded, taking a slow sip of his drink.

Abuelito: *"You know, when I was your age, I tried to hide parts of myself too. I wanted to fit in so badly that I ignored the things that made me, well... me. But the thing about hiding who you are? It doesn't make you fit in. It just makes you disappear."*

Michael swallowed, staring down at his blank page.

Michael: *"But it's hard, Abuelito. It'd be easier if I just... looked like everyone else."*

Abuelito reached out and gently tapped the table.

Abuelito: *"Mijo, looking like everyone else means nothing if it costs you who you really are. Your story, your history, your heart—that's what makes you special. Don't let anyone make you feel small for carrying those things."*

His words settled deep into Michael's chest.

For the first time, Michael started to see his project differently. Maybe this wasn't about fitting in. Maybe this was about showing up *as himself.*

Michael sat at his desk, staring at his sketchbook. The conversation with Abuelito had settled deep in his chest, filling him with something he hadn't felt in a while—pride.

He flipped open to a fresh page and picked up his pencil. This time, he didn't hesitate.

He started with his face, his features, but then he went deeper. He sketched the old soccer jersey Abuelito had given him, the one from his home country that still smelled faintly of grass and leather. He added the bold patterns he'd seen on the walls of his grandparents' house, weaving them into the background like a tapestry of his heritage.

With every line, every stroke, the image became more than just a school project. It was a statement—a reminder that he wasn't just one thing. He wasn't just another kid in school, trying to blend in.

"I'm more than just one thing," Michael thought, his pencil pressing firmly into the paper. *"I'm the stories, the music, the traditions. This is who I am. And if others don't get it... that's okay."*

For the first time in weeks, he felt peace.

The next day, Michael walked into Mr. Alvarez's classroom, his sketchbook tucked under his arm.

Mr. Alvarez glanced at his work and his eyes lit up.

Mr. Alvarez: *"Michael, this is incredible. You didn't just draw yourself—you told a story."*

Michael felt warmth spread in his chest.

Michael: (grinning) *"Thanks. I guess I just... stopped trying to make it look like something other people wanted."*

His teacher nodded. *"That's when the best work happens."*

Michael smiled. It wasn't a loud moment, but it was a win.

The next week, Mr. Alvarez announced that their class would be presenting their art work. Michael felt a flicker of hesitation.

Sure, he was proud of his work—but was he ready to stand in front of everyone and show them the real him?

Then, Abuelito's words came back to him.

"Looking like everyone else means nothing if it costs you who you really are."

So when the day of the presentations arrived, Michael didn't back down.

He stood in front of the class, gripping his drawing with both hands. He saw curious glances, whispers, a few classmates craning their necks to see his work.

He took a deep breath.

Michael: *"For a long time, I thought I had to look a certain way to fit in. But I've started to see that who I am isn't just about appearances. It's about the things I carry with me—my family, my culture, my experiences."*

He lifted his drawing higher.

Michael: *"This is me. Not just what's on the outside, but everything that makes me who I am."*

The room was silent for a moment. Then, one voice broke through. Ryan. The same Ryan who had made that comment in the hallway.

But this time, his voice wasn't mocking. Ryan: *"That's actually pretty cool."* Michael blinked.

Then, another classmate spoke up. David: *"Dude, that's solid. You put a lot into it."*

A few other students murmured their agreement. Even Mr. Alvarez looked proud. Mhael let out a slow breath.

They got it. Maybe not all of them, maybe not completely—but enough. And that was more than he ever expected. He walked back to his seat, feeling lighter.

For the first time, he wasn't just seen. He was understood.

At the art event, Michael stood at the front of the classroom, gripping his drawing. His heart pounded as he took a deep breath, preparing to say the words he had kept inside for too long.

Michael: *"For a long time, I thought I had to look a certain way to fit in. But I've realized that what I see in the mirror isn't just about looks. It's my family, my culture, my experiences. It's who I am."*

A silence settled over the room.

Michael felt the weight of uncertainty pressing down on him. Would they get it? Would they understand?

Then, Ryan, the same guy who had made a sarcastic comment weeks ago, nodded slightly.

Ryan: *"That's actually kinda cool, man."*

Michael blinked.

Then, another voice.

David: *"Yeah, I never really thought about it that way."*

Michael exhaled slowly. He hadn't expected applause. He hadn't expected a huge, dramatic moment.

But this? This meant something.

For the first time, he felt seen—not just as a kid in the background, but as himself.

In the days following his presentation, Michael noticed small but important changes.

When he looked in the mirror, he didn't feel like something was missing. He didn't compare himself to the guys at school who dressed differently or styled their hair a certain way.

He saw himself—whole, confident, enough.

One afternoon, as he scrolled through social media, he came across a post filled with the same images that used to make him doubt himself.

But this time? He just scrolled past. No pressure. No second-guessing. Just acceptance.

"I don't need to look like anyone else," he thought. *"Because my story—my identity—is already enough."*

And that realization?

It changed everything.

Michael hadn't set out to inspire anyone. But little by little, he saw it happening around him.

One day, at lunch, his friend Adam sat down across from him, looking thoughtful.

Adam: *"You know, after your project, I started thinking about my own family's history. My grandpa came here from the Philippines, and I've never really asked him about it. I guess... I just never thought about it like that."*

Michael smirked.

Michael: *"Dude, you should ask him. I bet he's got some cool stories."*

Adam nodded. And just like that, Michael realized something huge.

This whole time, he thought his journey was just about him—his struggle, his self-doubt, his acceptance.

But it wasn't.

By embracing who he was, he had given others permission to do the same.

As Michael walked through school that afternoon, he noticed something that made him smile. A few of his classmates had made small but meaningful changes—a wristband from their home country, a soccer jersey from their heritage, even a language textbook on their desk. Little pieces of who they were—pieces they had once kept hidden.

Michael realized that this journey was never about changing to meet anyone's expectations.

It was about finally seeing himself as whole—and showing others that they could be, too.

Learning Lessons from "Roots of Confidence"

Michael's journey teaches us that staying true to yourself is an act of strength.

It's easy to think you need to change to fit in, but your identity—your heritage, your story—is already enough. Finding the right people—friends, family, mentors—can remind you of your worth when you start to doubt yourself.

True confidence doesn't come from comparing yourself to others—it comes from embracing who you are. And finally, being yourself isn't just about you—it has the power to inspire others to do the same.

Michael's story proves that you don't have to fit a mold to belong. You just have to be you. And that's more than enough.

Story 9 - Unfolding Confidence

Lucas's bedroom was his retreat—a quiet place filled with half-finished sketches, stacks of comic books, and the faint scent of pencil shavings. His desk was cluttered with notebooks, his favorite markers, and doodles of characters he'd created. Here, he could be himself.

At school, things were different. Lucas wasn't the loudest kid in the room. He wasn't the guy making jokes at lunch or the one dominating the basketball court. He preferred to blend in—just another kid in jeans, a hoodie, and sneakers, keeping his head down.

Most people didn't even know he could draw. And that was fine with him.

But lately, something had started to change.

That night, Lucas lay on his bed, scrolling through his phone. He wasn't expecting much—just the usual mix of memes and game clips—when he saw a photo of Josh Kingston, one of the most popular guys at school.

Josh was at a weekend event, surrounded by friends, laughing in that easy, confident way of his. Everything about him—the way he dressed, the way he carried himself—seemed so effortless.

Lucas stared at the screen. Josh was the kind of guy people noticed.

Lucas, on the other hand? Not so much.

He set his phone down and caught a glimpse of himself in the mirror across the room. Messy brown hair. Ink-smudged fingers. The same hoodie he always wore.

"What do people even see when they look at me?"

For the first time, Lucas started to wonder if blending in was actually holding him back.

The next day, Lucas sat at his usual table in the cafeteria, absentmindedly sketching in the margins of his notebook while his friends talked around him.

But his ears tuned in when he heard a voice from a few tables away.

Josh and his friends were laughing, talking about something.

"All I'm saying is, confidence is everything," Josh was saying. *"You can tell when a guy has it. The way they walk, the way they dress… Some people just have that it factor."*

Lucas's stomach twisted.

Do I have that?

He glanced down at himself. Same old hoodie. Same scuffed sneakers. Same everything.

Would someone like Josh ever see him as confident?

Across the table, his best friend, Mateo, nudged him. *"Dude, you've been weirdly quiet today. What's up?"*

Lucas forced a small laugh. *"Just thinking."*

Mateo raised an eyebrow. *"Dangerous. Don't hurt yourself."* Lucas smirked but didn't respond. Because the truth was, he was caught in a thought he couldn't shake:

"Maybe if I changed how I looked—just a little—people would take me more seriously."

Maybe Josh was right.

That night, Lucas stood in front of his mirror, trying something new.

He ran some gel through his hair, flattening it instead of letting it do its usual messy thing. He pulled on a jacket instead of his hoodie, testing the look.

It felt... different.

Maybe this would help. Maybe it would make him look cooler, sharper, more confident. But something about it felt wrong. He frowned, staring at his reflection.

"Am I really willing to change this much just to fit in?"

The thought sat heavy in his chest.

After a long pause, he sighed and messed his hair back up, shrugging back into his hoodie. Something inside him wasn't ready to let go of himself—but the doubt was still there, creeping in like a shadow.

As Lucas lay in bed that night, his mind raced.

He picked up his sketchbook, flipping through his drawings. They had always been his escape, his way of expressing himself.

But for the first time, he wasn't sure if it was enough.

Would people ever notice him for who he really was? Or would he have to change just to be seen?

Lucas sat on the edge of his bed, his phone lying face-up beside him, the screen still glowing. His mind was a mess.

Everywhere he looked—on social media, at school—guys like Josh Kingston seemed to have it all together. They didn't just fit in; they stood out. They had confidence. They had presence.

And Lucas? He had a stack of sketchbooks filled with characters no one ever saw.

His fingers traced the cover of his current notebook, the edges worn soft from use. It had always been his escape—his way of expressing himself, of making sense of the world.

But now, as he flipped to a blank page, his hand froze.

"What if I changed a little? What if I dressed differently? Walked differently? Would they see me then?"

He tapped his pencil absently against the page, frustration bubbling in his chest.

"Am I really willing to change myself just to fit in?"

A part of him said no. But another part whispered back:

"What if fitting in is the only way to be noticed?"

With a sigh, he closed the sketchbook and set it aside, the pages a quiet reminder of who he was—a reminder he wasn't sure he was ready to let go of.

The next afternoon, Lucas lingered in the art room long after class ended.

The walls were covered in paintings and sketches—pieces left unfinished, ideas waiting to be fully realized. The air smelled like paper, paint, and creativity.

It should have been his favorite place in the world.

But today, it only made him feel stuck.

He had barely noticed his teacher, Mr. Calloway, as he sorted through a stack of brushes. An older man, with paint always on his hands and the kind of easy confidence that made people listen when he spoke.

"Lucas," he said, not looking up. *"Can you give me a hand with these?"*

Lucas nodded, grateful for a distraction. As they stacked jars of paint, they worked in comfortable silence—until Mr. Calloway glanced at him with a knowing look.

"You're quiet today," he said. *"More than usual."*

Lucas shrugged, not sure how to explain what was going on in his head.

But Mr. Calloway wasn't the type to let things slide.

"You know, when I was your age," he continued, *"I spent way too much time trying to be like everyone else."* He chuckled to himself. *"Thought I had to dress the right way, talk the right way, even pretend I liked things I didn't—just to fit in."*

Lucas hesitated, his grip tightening on a jar of blue paint.

Mr. Calloway's voice softened. *"Took me a while to realize something: the people who actually matter? They notice the real you. Not the version you pretend to be."*

Lucas stared at the row of paint jars in front of him, something tightening in his chest.

He wanted to believe that. He really did.

But... what if he was too plain to stand out?

"What if being myself just isn't enough?" he muttered, the words slipping out before he could stop them.

Mr. Calloway set down the paintbrush he was holding. *"Lucas, confidence doesn't come from becoming someone else. It comes from realizing you already have something unique—something no one else can copy. When you believe that? Others will see it too."*

Lucas looked down at his hands, streaked with paint, and let the words sink in.

Lucas didn't respond right away. He wasn't sure what to say. But as he left the art room that afternoon, he felt a little different.

Like maybe, just maybe, there was a way to stand out without losing himself.

As Lucas took in Mr. Calloway's words, something inside him shifted—a quiet reassurance, like the first brushstroke on a blank canvas.

His eyes wandered to the paint-splattered shelves around the art room, the vibrant colors reminding him of the sketches he had kept hidden away. The ones that felt like pieces of himself.

"He makes it sound so simple," Lucas thought, doubt still lingering in the back of his mind. *"But... what if he's right?"*

For the first time in days, Lucas felt a flicker of hope, like he was finally seeing himself in a different light.

That night, as he stood in front of his mirror, he made a small but meaningful choice.

Instead of trying to pick out clothes that would make him blend in, he reached for his favorite hoodie—the one that felt like home. He ruffled his hair instead of slicking it back. He grabbed his sketchbook, sliding it into his backpack, even though part of him still hesitated.

Looking at his reflection, he noticed something—a sense of calm he hadn't felt in a long time.

"Maybe I don't have to change everything to stand out," he thought. *"Maybe just being me... is enough to start with."*

At school the next morning, Lucas walked through the crowded hallway, his sketchbook tucked under his arm.

His friends gave him a quick once-over but didn't say much. He could tell they noticed, though.

A couple of classmates threw him curious glances. But for the first time, he didn't look away. Instead, he met their eyes with quiet confidence and kept walking, his grip on his sketchbook steady.

During art class, Mr. Calloway noticed. He gave Lucas a small nod—a silent acknowledgment of his first step forward.

Lucas slid into his seat and opened his sketchbook, letting his pencil move freely across the page. For the first time in weeks, it felt right.

Across the table, Jordan, a kid from class who usually stuck to himself, leaned over slightly.

"I didn't know you drew like that," Jordan said, eyes flicking to the sketch. *"That's... actually really cool."*

Lucas hesitated, then smiled—just a little. *"Thanks,"* he said. *"It's just something I enjoy."*

And in that moment, he realized: this small choice—showing up as himself—was a powerful beginning.

And maybe, just maybe, it was enough.

Lucas walked into the hallway, still riding the small but important victory of the morning.

But confidence was a fragile thing, and it didn't take long for the first real test to hit.

As he passed by a group of students near the lockers, he caught a glance from Ryan Kingston—one of the guys who always seemed to be effortlessly cool.

Ryan raised an eyebrow, nudging his friend before stepping into Lucas's path.

Ryan smirked. *"New look, Lucas? Trying to go for that 'deep artist' vibe now?"*

His friend chuckled beside him. Lucas felt his grip on his sketchbook tighten. For a moment, doubt crept in again.

"Do I really stand out this much... and is that a bad thing? What if I really don't belong anywhere?"

But then, he heard another voice—his own.

"This is supposed to be about me, not them."

Just then, Jordan, the same classmate from art, walked by. He noticed the exchange, then shot Lucas a nod.

"Forget them, man," he said casually, as if it wasn't even a question. *"They don't get it."*

Lucas exhaled, some of the tension in his chest easing. He didn't say anything to Ryan. He didn't need to.

Instead, he walked past, his grip on his sketchbook steady. For the first time, he didn't feel like he had to apologize for being himself.

It wasn't what Ryan said that bothered him—it was the way he said it. The slight smirk. The casual dismissal.

Lucas tightened his grip on his sketchbook, his fingers pressing into the cover.

"Why does this still get to me?"

His thoughts swirled.

"Thanks," Lucas muttered. *"Sometimes, I don't even know if I'm doing this for me... or if I just want to prove something to everyone else."*

Jordan shrugged. *"Maybe it's both. And maybe that's okay. Just don't forget—there's more to you than what people see."*

His words settled over Lucas like a steadying force.

As he walked to his next class, Lucas held his sketchbook a little more confidently, reminding himself that this journey had never been about them—it was about him.

The school courtyard buzzed with laughter and conversation.

Lucas had found a quiet corner, flipping through his sketchbook, getting lost in the lines and shading. But then—a voice cut through the background noise.

He looked up. Carter—the guy everyone seemed to admire—was standing across the courtyard, laughing with Ryan and a few others.

And beside him? Mason.

Mason was the kind of guy Lucas had once thought he could be. The kind who was always at ease, effortlessly cool, the guy people naturally gravitated toward.

Lucas watched as Carter leaned in, clearly engaged in whatever Mason was saying.

It was like Lucas wasn't even in the same world.

His grip on his pencil slackened. *"He doesn't even notice me."*

The self-assurance Lucas had been building felt like it was slipping away.

"Maybe I'll never be the type of guy people notice. Maybe this is just who I am—someone who blends into the background."

Lucas felt the pull to change again for the first time since starting this journey. To mold himself into what he thought Carter—and maybe everyone else—wanted him to be.

His confidence, once solid, now felt fragile, like a candle flickering in the wind.

Yet even as he sat there, wrestling with self-doubt, something inside him resisted.

A small, steady voice reminded him:

"You didn't come this far just to erase yourself again."

And although he couldn't fully silence the doubt, he made a choice:

He left the courtyard without altering himself. But he knew the hardest test was still ahead.

The night of the school social arrived, and Lucas stood in front of his mirror, barely recognizing himself.

Instead of his usual hoodie, he wore a stiff button-up, his hair styled like the guys he used to admire.

He had listened to his friends. He had followed their advice.

But now, as he stared at his reflection... something felt off.

He adjusted his collar, then ran a hand through his hair, trying to shake the unease.

"Maybe this is what it takes. Maybe this is what I need to do to finally be noticed."

But as he looked into his own eyes, a question lingered:

"If I walk into that room like this... am I still me?"

Lucas stepped into the crowded school event, the lights flashing, music pulsing. He had spent time making sure his outfit was right— not his usual hoodie and jeans, but something more "put-together," something that looked like what Carter and the other guys wore.

At first, he thought the change would make him feel different— stronger, more confident.

But now, standing there, he just felt... wrong.

His new clothes were stiff, the styled hair wasn't really him, and the casual, effortless confidence he had hoped for? It never came.

Then, he spotted Carter across the room, laughing with his friends, completely comfortable—not because of what he was wearing, but because he wasn't trying to be anyone else.

"They're not thinking about what they look like."

"They're just having fun, being themselves."

And suddenly, it clicked. Lucas had spent all this time believing he had to change to be noticed, to fit in. But real confidence wasn't about trying to be like them.

It was about being comfortable in his own skin.

With a deep breath, he slipped into the bathroom, gripping the edges of the sink as he stared at his reflection.

Who was he trying to impress? Carter? Ryan? His classmates?

Did their approval even matter if it meant losing himself?

He exhaled sharply, ran his hands through his overly styled hair— messing it up into something more him—and pulled off the jacket that never felt right.

The weight of pretense lifted.

When he stepped back into the event, it wasn't to prove anything. It was just to enjoy the night—as himself.

The next morning, Lucas walked into school feeling... different. Not because he had done something dramatic. But because, he wasn't second-guessing himself.

He wore his favorite hoodie, his sneakers—the ones that were worn down but comfortable.

His sketchbook was tucked under his arm. Not to hide it, not to prove anything, but simply because he wanted it with him.

He walked down the hallway, noticing how easy it felt to just... be.

Then, he spotted Jordan heading his way. Jordan's eyes flicked over him, and he smirked. *"Dude, I don't know what it is, but you look... more like you."*

Lucas chuckled. *"Thanks. I guess I just realized... if someone doesn't like me as I am, then maybe they're not my people."*

Jordan grinned and fist-bumped him. *"Now that's what I'm talking about."*

Lucas felt a quiet satisfaction settle in.

He had spent so much time worrying about standing out in the wrong way.

Now?

He didn't care if he stood out or blended in. He was just being Lucas. And that was enough.

That afternoon, Lucas sat at his desk, staring at a blank page.

His English teacher had assigned a personal project on identity— something real, something honest.

Lucas knew he had plenty to say. But putting his journey into words— laying out the self-doubt, the struggle, the realization that he didn't need to change to be enough— that was terrifying.

Would people judge him? Would they think less of him if they knew how much he had struggled?

His fingers hovered over the page. Then, he glanced at his sketchbook.

The worn edges, the pages filled with drawings that reflected pieces of himself.

A reminder of who he really was.

A small smile tugged at his lips.

"If I share this... maybe someone else will feel less alone."

With a deep breath, he picked up his pen and started writing.

He wrote about trying to fit into a mold, about the feeling of standing on the outside, about wanting to be noticed but realizing he didn't need to change to be seen.

When he finished, he read the title:

"Learning to Be Me."

And for the first time, he felt ready to share his story.

The day of Lucas's presentation arrived.

He stood at the front of the classroom, his palms slightly sweaty.

He wasn't used to opening up like this.

Taking a deep breath, he began to read. At first, his voice was uncertain, but as he continued, something shifted.

The words felt real—honest.

He shared how he had struggled with self-doubt, how he had tried to fit into expectations that weren't really his own, and how he had finally learned that his worth wasn't based on how others saw him— but on how he saw himself.

As he spoke, the nervousness faded.

By the time he reached the last line, he felt something new—a quiet, steady confidence.

When he finished, the room was silent for a moment.

Then, a few classmates nodded in quiet understanding. From the back of the room, Jordan gave him a nod of approval.

After class, Lucas was heading to lunch when Carter approached him.

Carter shuffled his feet a little, his usual easy confidence softened. *"Hey, Lucas... I just wanted to say that your presentation was..."* He hesitated, then shrugged. *"...Really cool. I mean, I get what you were saying. I think a lot of us do."*

Lucas blinked. He hadn't expected that.

"Yeah?" he asked.

Carter nodded. *"Yeah. I mean... I don't think I've ever said it out loud, but sometimes I feel like I gotta act a certain way too, y'know?"*

Lucas felt a warmth settle in his chest.

This wasn't just about his journey anymore. He had helped someone else see things differently too.

Over the next few days, Lucas noticed something strange. His classmates looked at him a little differently now. Not in the way he used to fear—not with judgment, but with respect.

They saw him not as someone who had tried to fit in—but as someone who had learned to stand on his own.

And that felt better than any approval he had once craved.

One afternoon, Lucas sat outside during lunch, sketchbook open, doodling absentmindedly.

Jordan plopped down next to him.

"You're not gonna start giving motivational speeches now, are you?" he teased with a smirk.

Lucas chuckled. "Nah. But... I guess I just get it now."

"Get what?" Jordan asked.

"That I never had to change," Lucas said simply. "I just had to be okay with who I already was."

Jordan nodded. "Yeah. I think people are starting to get that too."

Lucas smiled. This journey hadn't just changed him—it had changed the people around him.

He had returned to where he started—but he wasn't the same.

Now, he knew his worth.

Not because anyone told him.

But because he had finally told himself.

Learning Lessons from "Unfolding Confidence"

Lucas's journey reminds us that true confidence comes from within, not from changing yourself to meet others' expectations.

It's easy to feel the pressure to act a certain way, dress a certain way, or fit into a specific mold to be accepted. But Lucas's story proves that authenticity is more powerful than imitation.

By sharing his struggles, Lucas helped his classmates realize they weren't alone. Sometimes, being real gives others the courage to do the same.

Instead of trying to impress people who valued appearances, upi can find that true friends respect you for who you are, not for who you pretend to be.

The world doesn't need another copy of someone else. It needs you— exactly as you are.

Story 10 - True Style

Early in his teens, Noah moves through the familiar rhythm of school, hanging out with his close friends, and escaping into his creative passion—customizing sneakers.

At home, his small sneaker workshop is his sanctuary, a place where he can experiment with designs, colors, and unique patterns that reflect his personality. Each custom sneaker he works on feels like an extension of his creativity, and he imagines one day wearing them with confidence.

But at school, Noah's world feels restrictive. Most of his friends are into big-name sneaker brands, wearing the latest Air Jordans, Yeezys, and Nikes they see all over social media. Noah doesn't feel like he can pull off those looks with the same ease. Instead, he sticks to his plain sneakers, hoodies, and jeans, choosing comfort but at the cost of feeling overlooked.

On a Saturday afternoon, Noah sits cross-legged on his bedroom floor, flipping through a sneaker magazine his friend let him borrow. The pages are filled with the latest high-end shoes—sleek designs, bright colors, and big logos that make him feel a mix of admiration and frustration.

He sets the magazine aside and picks up a sneaker he's been working on, carefully painting a blue-and-orange lightning pattern along the side. He glances at his reflection in the mirror, holding the shoe next to his worn-out sneakers, and imagines walking into school wearing them. But then doubt creeps in.

"Would people actually think these are cool? Or would they just think they look weird?"

On Monday, as Noah steps into the bustling cafeteria, he catches his friends excitedly talking about the upcoming school basketball game. They're discussing what they'll wear, especially the sneakers they're planning to show off.

One of his friends, Jordan, pulls out his phone, showing off a pair of brand-new, limited-edition Jordans that he's saving up for.

Jordan: *"Noah, what are you wearing to the game? You always talk about sneaker designs—you should get a fresh pair."*

Noah: *"Oh, uh... I haven't really thought about it yet."*

Mason: *"Dude, you literally design sneakers all the time. You should wear one of your own to the game!"*

For a second, Noah feels a rush of excitement. The basketball game could be an opportunity to finally show his work—to wear something that's completely his. But then doubt creeps in again.

"What if people think they look ridiculous? What if I just stand out in a bad way?"

Noah looks at Jordan's sleek, name-brand sneakers and suddenly feels small.

Later that evening, Noah sits at his desk, staring at the sneakers he designed. Beside them, his notebook lies open, filled with sketches of bold, colorful designs.

He picks up one of the custom sneakers and studies it in the dim light, feeling torn between excitement and doubt.

"Am I really brave enough to wear these? What if they don't look right? What if people just laugh?"

Noah sighs and slides the sneakers under his bed, pushing them out of sight.

"Maybe it's just easier to wear something normal."

With that decision, he turns away from his creativity, choosing to blend in rather than stand out.

The next day, Noah's art teacher, Mr. Castillo, catches him as class is wrapping up. Mr. Castillo is one of the coolest teachers at school— he's got this way of making art feel effortless and bold. Whether it's his paint-splattered sneakers or the way he customizes his denim jacket, he stands out without even trying. Noah has always admired that about him.

As the last few students head out, the room settles into a quiet hum of creativity—dried paint on palettes, sketchbooks left open, half-finished projects waiting to be completed. Mr. Castillo turns to Noah with an easygoing smile.

Mr. Castillo: *"Hey, Noah. You've been quiet lately. Everything good?"*

Noah hesitates, gripping his plain white sneaker under the desk. *"Yeah, I guess. Just thinking a lot."*

Mr. Castillo leans against the desk, studying him thoughtfully. *"Thinking about what?"*

Noah sighs. *"It's just... I design sneakers all the time, but I feel like I can't actually wear them. Like... what if they're too different? Everyone at school is into big brands and limited-edition stuff. I don't think my designs would ever fit in."*

Mr. Castillo tilts his head. *"And? Since when is art about fitting in?"*

Noah blinks, caught off guard. *"I mean... I don't know. It's just easier to blend in."*

Mr. Castillo chuckles, shaking his head. *"Noah, art isn't about blending in. It's about standing out."* He nods toward the sneakers peeking from under Noah's desk. *"And those? Those are yours. No brand name, no mass production—just you. That's what makes them cool."*

Noah feels a mix of doubt and curiosity. He wants to believe Mr. Castillo, but confidence doesn't come that easily. *"Yeah, but what if people think they're weird?"*

Mr. Castillo grins. *"You ever notice how the coolest people are the ones who don't care what anyone else thinks?"*

Noah lets that sink in. He's never thought about it that way.

That night, Noah sits in his room, staring at the sneakers he designed. The bold blue-and-orange lightning streaks stand out against the plain white canvas.

Beside him, his notebook is open to a page filled with sketches of custom designs—each one more unique than the last. His fingers hover over the shoe, tracing the painted edges.

Mr. Castillo's words echo in his mind - *"Since when is art about fitting in?"*

Noah glances at his closet, where his usual plain sneakers sit untouched. Safe. Ordinary.

He exhales slowly, then laces up his custom sneakers. They feel different on his feet. Not just comfortable—real. Like he's finally stepping into something that's his.

Noah stands in front of the mirror. The sneakers pop against his usual hoodie and jeans. They're different. They're bold.

His heart beats a little faster as he imagines walking into school with them. He can already picture the curious glances, the possible stares.

But then he straightens his shoulders.

"Okay," he thinks, *"they're just sneakers... but they're mine. Maybe this is a start."*

With one last deep breath, Noah grabs his backpack, steps out of his room, and heads for the door—taking his first real step toward owning his identity.

With his custom sneakers laced up, Noah feels a small but real spark of confidence. They aren't like the expensive brand-name shoes most guys at school wear, but they feel more him than anything else.

But the moment he steps into the crowded hallway, that confidence starts to crack.

He catches a few quick glances, hears a couple of whispered comments. His gut twists as he wonders if he made a mistake.

At his locker, he overhears Dylan, one of the more popular guys in school, snickering with his friend.

Dylan smirks, looking down at Noah's sneakers. *"New kicks, Noah? What, you designing your own brand now?"*

Noah keeps his voice steady. *"Just thought I'd try something different."*

Dylan raises an eyebrow. *"Yeah, well... it's definitely different."* He scoffs before walking off, his friend chuckling beside him.

Noah grits his teeth, gripping the strap of his backpack. The sneakers that felt bold and exciting this morning now feel like a target.

Just then, his friend Lucas steps up next to him.

Lucas glances at the sneakers and grins. *"Dude, those are sick. You made these?"*

Noah nods, shifting slightly. *"Yeah... just something I've been messing around with."*

Lucas nods approvingly. *"That's awesome, man. I mean, anyone can buy Jordans, but these? No one else has these."*

Noah exhales, his shoulders relaxing slightly. Lucas's support softens the sting of Dylan's comment. Even though doubt still lingers, he's not completely alone in this.

As he watches Dylan and his friends blend into the crowd, a thought tugs at him.

"Why does being myself have to feel so hard? Wouldn't it just be easier to blend in?"

But then he looks down at his sneakers.

"I made these. They mean something to me. Do I really want to trade that just to fit in?"

For the first time, he doesn't have a clear answer.

Later that week, Noah finds himself at a friend's house for a small gathering. He hesitated to come, worried about standing out, but decided to go anyway.

As he steps inside, he immediately notices Jake—one of the most effortlessly cool guys in their grade.

Jake is joking around with a few friends, his brand-new Nikes standing out—sleek, expensive, and exactly the kind of thing everyone at school seems to want.

Noah glances down at his own sneakers, the ones he designed and painted himself. They suddenly feel like a spotlight on his feet, making him stand out in a way he isn't sure he likes.

Across the room, Dylan is talking with a group, his voice loud and confident.

Noah shifts near the door, adjusting the cuff of his jeans as if that might somehow make the sneakers less noticeable. He catches Dylan's glance for a split second and sees the amused smirk return.

Then Dylan nudges Jake and says, *"Man, those Nikes are clean. Real shoes."*

Jake grins. *"Gotta keep it fresh."*

Noah feels his stomach drop.

He suddenly feels like an outsider in a room where everyone else seems to fit in so easily.

A thought crosses his mind, heavy and full of doubt.

"Maybe I'll never be the kind of guy who fits in without trying. Why do I have to feel so different?"

Noah feels tempted to conform completely. Maybe he should just go home, take off the sneakers, and stick to safe choices. No more designs. No more attention. Just fitting in.

But is that what he really wants?

Later that evening, Noah is getting ready for a family gathering.

His mom glances at him as he hesitates in front of his closet.

Mom: *"You okay, bud?"*

Noah shrugs, running a hand through his hair. *"Yeah. Just thinking about what to wear."*

His mom raises an eyebrow. *"That's new."*

Noah exhales. *"It's just... I don't know. I guess I don't want to look weird."*

His mom gives him a knowing look. *"You mean you don't want to stand out."*

Noah doesn't respond. That's exactly what he means.

She steps closer and gently rests a hand on his shoulder.

Mom: *"You know, confidence isn't about looking like everyone else. It's about feeling good in your own skin."*

Noah nods slowly but still feels unsure.

After a pause, he looks toward his desk, where his latest sneaker design sits—one he hasn't worn yet. It's a mix of bold colors and patterns, a true reflection of his creativity.

His fingers hover over it.

A choice.

Play it safe... or take a risk?

Finally, with a steadying breath, he reaches for the sneakers.

This time, he's choosing to own his style.

Noah steps into his uncle's house, his custom sneakers firmly on his feet. He feels a mix of pride and uncertainty—this is the first time he's worn them to a big family gathering.

As he scans the room, he spots his older cousin Jordan near the snack table.

Jordan, always dressed in the latest gear, glances at Noah's sneakers. His smirk is subtle but sharp.

Jordan: *"Whoa, custom kicks? Didn't know you were starting a fashion line, man."*

Noah's stomach drops. His fingers briefly tighten around his phone in his pocket, an old habit when he feels nervous.

The sting of Jordan's words settles deep, and for a second, the urge to blend in resurfaces.

He almost looks down at his sneakers—almost second-guesses himself.

But then, across the room, he sees his dad watching with a quiet, approving nod.

Noah takes a slow breath. *"Why does Jordan's opinion hit so hard? I designed these because I love them. Why should I need his approval to feel like myself?"*

Instead of hiding his feet behind the couch or making a self-deprecating joke, Noah simply straightens his shoulders and lets his hand fall away from his pocket.

Jordan raises an eyebrow, expecting Noah to laugh along with him.

But Noah just shrugs. *"Yeah, man. I like 'em."*

It's a simple statement. But it feels big.

Jordan watches him for a second longer, then just nods and moves on, grabbing a soda from the counter.

The moment passes, but for Noah, it means something. He made the choice not to shrink.

The next morning, Noah wakes up feeling lighter. He doesn't second-guess what he's going to wear.

He pulls on a hoodie he designed himself, one he'd always liked but never dared to wear to school. Paired with his sneakers, it feels like a statement—but not one for anyone else.

This time, he's wearing it for himself.

At lunch, as he steps toward his usual table, Lucas and Ethan immediately take notice.

Lucas: *"Dude, that hoodie is sick. You make that?"*

Ethan: *"Bro, why didn't you ever wear this stuff before? You've got actual style."*

Noah grins, a little surprised at how natural the compliments feel.

Noah: *"Guess I finally stopped overthinking it."*

Ethan shakes his head with a laugh. *"Man, if I could design stuff like that, I'd wear it all the time."*

As his friends continue to talk, Noah realizes something:

His self-expression isn't just about him anymore.

By being confident in his own style, he's inspiring the people around him, too.

Later that week, Noah's English teacher, Mr. Reynolds, announces a project.

Mr. Reynolds: *"For this assignment, I want you all to create something that represents who you are. It can be a speech, a design, a song, anything that expresses your individuality."*

Noah feels a flicker of hesitation. Sharing his story feels vulnerable.

The idea of explaining why he started designing his own clothes—how he used to feel invisible, how he almost gave up on his creativity just to fit in—feels like opening up too much.

But then, he glances down at his hoodie.

And a thought solidifies.

"Maybe this project isn't just about me."

Maybe this is his chance to fully step into who he's becoming. Maybe it's time to own his story.

That night, Noah sits at his desk, his sketchbook open and pencils scattered.

He's spent the past hour working on a custom hoodie design— something that represents not just his love for streetwear, but his journey of self-acceptance.

The page slowly fills with bold lettering, unique graphics, and color accents that tell his story.

He pauses, tapping his pencil against the desk, a wave of doubt creeping in.

"Am I really ready to show this to everyone? What if they don't get it? What if they think it's dumb?"

His fingers hover over the edge of the page, almost tempted to rip it out, to hide it like before.

But then, he thinks back to everything that's led him here—to the sneakers he designed, to the hoodie he finally had the confidence to wear, to the moment he didn't let Jordan's smirk define him.

And for now, he doesn't let the doubt win.

Noah takes a deep breath, flips his pencil around, and boldly writes the title at the top of the page:

"True Identity."

When the day arrives for Noah to present his project, his hands feel just a little sweaty, but there's also a steady confidence he didn't have before.

Standing at the front of the classroom, he holds up his design—a fully realized hoodie concept, complete with sketches, details, and the meaning behind each element.

His voice is shaky at first, but as he explains the journey behind it—how he used to feel invisible, how he thought he had to dress a certain way to fit in, how designing his own style made him feel like himself—his voice grows stronger.

The classroom falls silent as he speaks.

He takes a steadying breath, glancing at his design and then at his classmates.

Noah: *"I used to think confidence came from wearing what was popular. But I've realized confidence comes from wearing something that feels like you. This hoodie? This design? It's mine. And that's what makes it cool."*

As he finishes, he glances up—his friend Lucas is grinning, Ethan gives him a nod, and even some classmates who never talked to him before seem impressed.

Ben, a kid from the back row who always seemed effortlessly cool, raises an eyebrow and leans forward.

Ben: *"Dude, that's actually fire. Are you gonna make it for real?"*

Noah blinks. He wasn't expecting that.

Noah: *"Uh... maybe."*

Lucas smirks. *"If you do, let me know—I'd wear one."*

A slow grin spreads across Noah's face. Maybe he didn't just share a project. Maybe... he changed the way people saw him.

At lunch, Noah's sitting with Lucas and Ethan when Jordan—his cousin—walks up.

Jordan shifts awkwardly before speaking.

Jordan: *"Hey... about that design you showed today. It was cool. I didn't know you were into that kind of thing."*

Noah studies him for a second. Jordan doesn't sound sarcastic. If anything, he sounds... a little impressed.

Noah shrugs, but there's an easy confidence in his voice now.

Noah: *"Yeah, man. It's what I do."*

Jordan nods and heads off, leaving Noah with a feeling he never expected—respect.

Not because he changed himself. But because he didn't.

Learning Lessons from "True Style"

Noah's journey shows that real confidence doesn't come from wearing what's popular—it comes from wearing what feels right to you.

At first, Noah thought he had to blend in to be accepted, but he realized that standing out is only scary if you're unsure of yourself. Once he embraced his unique style, others began to respect him—not because he followed trends, but because he was true to himself.

If you ever feel pressured to change who you are just to fit in, ask yourself: Are you doing it because you want to, or because you think you have to?

Whether it's wearing something different, sharing your talents, or speaking up for what you believe in, choosing to be yourself will always be worth it.

Story 11 - The Elixir

Mike's life is built on discipline, structure, and success.

From the outside, he's the guy who has it all together—top grades, the go-to leader for group projects, the first one to raise his hand in class. Teachers admire him. Parents praise him. Classmates respect him.

But beneath the surface, Mike's life is a constant balancing act, held together by the fear that if he messes up, even once, everything will fall apart.

Every morning, he wakes up to the sound of his alarm, his schedule carefully planned out. His desk is stacked with neatly arranged notebooks, his assignments completed ahead of time. He double-checks every detail, making sure nothing slips.

At school, he's known as the "perfectionist." While other kids celebrate a B+, Mike only sees a failure if it's not an A.

But lately, a new feeling has crept in—a growing unease. No matter how much he succeeds, it never feels enough.

One morning in English class, Mr. Carter, his teacher, announces a new project.

Mr. Carter: *"For your next assignment, I want you to write about a time you failed and what you learned from it."*

The class groans—but Mike freezes.

Failure? What failure?

His entire identity is built on avoiding mistakes.

His stomach tightens as the words sink in. He's spent years doing everything right, making sure there was never a moment of weakness. And now, he's expected to dig up something imperfect—and share it?

He grips his pencil tightly. *"I can't do this. I can't just let everyone see that I'm not as perfect as they think."*

That night, Mike stares at the blinking cursor on his laptop, paralyzed.

He tries to think of a failure, but every idea feels too small or too risky. He considers writing about the time he lost two points on a test—but that's not a real failure.

He hesitates, then slams his laptop shut.

"If I admit failure, does that mean I wasn't really good enough in the first place?"

For the first time in years, he feels stuck.

At the next class the following day, Mike grips his pencil tightly as Mr. Carter scans the classroom, his words hanging heavy in the air.

"Remember, this is a safe space. The point is to explore how challenges help us grow."

Safe? Mike doesn't feel safe at all.

The idea of writing about failure makes his chest tighten. It's like someone asking him to broadcast his worst moment to the whole world.

He nods stiffly, hoping to avoid attention, but inside, his mind is racing. *"I can't do this. I don't fail. I can't fail. What am I supposed to write? That time I got second place in a math competition? That barely counts."*

But there's no escape. The assignment is happening.

Mike feels like he's about to be exposed.

That night, Mike sits at his desk, staring at the glow of his laptop screen.

The cursor blinks, waiting. But his hands won't move.

He types a few words. *Deletes them.* Tries again. *Deletes them again.*

His room, usually a place of order and focus, suddenly feels too quiet. Too tight.

Stacks of notebooks sit untouched. His color-coded calendar, normally a source of control, now feels like it's mocking him.

"This is out of my hands. I can't plan my way out of this one. What if writing this ruins everything?"

His heartbeat quickens. He considers writing something safe—maybe the time he lost a few points on a quiz. That's failure, technically. Right?

But it's a lie. And he knows it.

Mike leans back in his chair, rubbing his face. The weight of expectation and fear presses down on him.

He feels lost, unsure of his next step.

The next day, Mike drags himself through school, feeling heavier than usual.

By the time English class ends, he's already halfway out the door when - "Mike, can you stay for a moment?"

Mr. Carter's voice is calm, but Mike stiffens. He hesitates, then slowly nods.

The classroom empties. The usual noise of students fades into silence.

Mr. Carter leans against his desk, arms relaxed. Not demanding—just waiting.

Mike shifts uncomfortably in his seat.

Mr. Carter: *"You've been quiet today. What's on your mind?"*

Mike stares at his hands.

Mike: *"It's this project. I don't know what to write. I... I don't fail."*

Mr. Carter nods, like he expected that answer.

Mr. Carter: *"I get it. But here's the thing—growth doesn't come from getting it right all the time. It comes from what you do when things don't go your way."*

Mike finally looks up.

Mike: *"But if I tell people I messed up... what if they don't see me the same way anymore?"*

Mr. Carter holds his gaze.

Mr. Carter: *"Then maybe they'll see you as human. And maybe that's not a bad thing."*

Mike doesn't respond.

However, for the first time, he contemplates that he may have been viewing this situation incorrectly.

Mike sits stiffly in his chair, watching as Mr. Carter leans against his desk.

Mr. Carter: *"Mike, real strength isn't about never messing up. It's about how you bounce back afterward. Let me tell you something— my first year teaching, I completely bombed a lesson. Total disaster. I felt like a failure."*

Mike blinks. Mr. Carter? Failing?

Mr. Carter: *"But you know what? That mistake taught me how to adapt. How to be better. That lesson sticks with me more than any success ever has."*

Mike frowns, gripping the edge of his desk. *"Failure... leading to something good? That's not how it works for me. If I mess up, I lose everything I've built."*

But still... Mr. Carter doesn't look weak admitting it. If anything, he seems more sure of himself.

Something shifts inside Mike—a small flicker of doubt about the way he's always seen failure.

That night, Mike sits at his desk, the glow of his laptop reflecting in his tense expression.

He hovers over the keyboard, fingers unmoving. *"I can't do this. If I write the truth, what if people look at me differently? What if they stop seeing me as the guy who's always on top?"*

His knee bounces under the desk. His brain tells him to pick something safe—like the time he forgot his homework at home. That's *technically* failure, right?

But then Mr. Carter's words replay in his mind. *"Real strength is how you bounce back."*

Mike exhales sharply. His fingers tighten into fists, then unclench.

Slowly, he starts typing.

He writes about the time he turned in an assignment late—something he's never told anyone. How it made him feel like he'd let himself down. How he dreaded his teacher's reaction.

Each sentence feels like lifting a weight he didn't even know he was carrying.

When he's finished, he leans back, staring at the screen.

It's not perfect. But it's real.

For a moment, things feel lighter. Mike starts to think, maybe being honest won't be so bad.

But then—

The Math Test.

Mike stares at the red 89% on his paper like it's a scarlet letter.

The numbers blur. His chest tightens. *"This is bad. This is really bad. People are going to notice."*

He grips the paper, his knuckles turning white as he slides into his seat.

Across the table, his friend Jordan glances over.

Jordan: *"Dude, an 89? That's awesome. I'd kill for that."*

Mike forces a weak chuckle, shoving the test into his backpack like it might disappear.

Mike: *"Yeah… it's fine."*

But inside? Mike thinks *"It's not fine. What if people think I'm slipping? What if I'm not the best anymore?"*

As the bell rings, he overhears whispers from the row behind him.

Ethan: *"Mike didn't get an A?"*

Lucas: *"Guess he's not as perfect as everyone thinks."*

The words slice through him.

He stares straight ahead, jaw clenched, hands fisting around his backpack straps.

"Everyone's noticing. They're already waiting for me to fall. If I'm not the best… what am I?"

The small victory from his essay vanishes.

Mike thought he was learning to handle imperfection—but now, standing in the wreckage of his own expectations, he's not so sure.

Mike keeps his head down as he walks into class, gripping his test paper so tightly the edges crumple. 89%.

Whispers float through the room.

Ethan: *"Mike didn't get an A? That's a first."*

Lucas: *"Guess even he can mess up."*

Each word hits like a body blow.

Mike clenches his jaw, shoulders going rigid. He pretends not to hear, but the words burrow deep.

Across the table, his friend Jordan nudges him.

Jordan: *"Dude, it's one test. No big deal."*

Mike forces a chuckle, stuffing the paper into his backpack like it's evidence of a crime.

Mike: *"Yeah... whatever."*

But inside, his mind is spinning - *"They noticed. I knew they would. One slip, and suddenly I'm not the guy who always has it together."*

The debate competition is coming.

It's the perfect way to prove—to himself, to everyone—that he's still the best.

But doubt gnaws at him.

His room, usually neat and controlled, is now a battlefield. Debate notes cover his desk. Crumpled flashcards litter the floor. His laptop screen glows with half-written arguments.

The soft hum of the desk lamp casts shadows under his eyes. He hasn't slept much.

He paces the room, gripping a flashcard, voice hoarse as he runs through his arguments for the hundredth time.

"If I don't get this perfect, what's the point? They'll see I'm slipping. They'll see I'm not as capable as they think."

His throat tightens. He collapses onto his bed, staring at the ceiling.

His phone buzzes—a dozen missed messages from friends.

He doesn't answer. His world shrinks to this singular goal: winning.

But then—A new thought creeps in. *"I'm so tired. How much longer can I keep this up?"*. He lets himself sit with the question.

He glances at his flashcards. Usually, he'd grab one. Start again.

But this time? His hands stay still.

The auditorium hums with anticipation.

Mike stands at the podium, notes clutched tight in one hand. He inhales sharply, scanning the crowd.

This is it. The moment he's worked himself to exhaustion for.

He starts strong. His voice is steady. His points are sharp. For a moment, he feels in control. And then—

He stumbles.

A key statistic slips from his mind. His words halt. The room shrinks. The silence closes in.

His pulse pounds in his ears. *"No. No, no, no. This can't be happening."*

He grips the podium, forcing his voice to steady. But it's too late. The mistake is out there.

And for the first time in his life, Mike has to face what happens when he isn't perfect.

Mike's hands grip the podium like a lifeline. His heart hammers against his ribs, his breath tight in his chest. *"Come on, Noah. Get it together."*

He forces himself to keep going. He takes a sharp inhale, steadies his voice, and pushes through. His words return, his points land, and he manages to finish strong.

A smattering of applause.

On the surface? He's held it together.

But inside? The stumble is all he can hear. The moment clings to him like a stain. *"That one mistake ruined it all. Why couldn't I just get it perfect?"*

Backstage, his body finally relaxes. Too much. He sinks onto a bench, hands trembling. The sounds of the auditorium fade into a dull hum.

The tension unravels all at once. His arms feel heavy. His mind, louder than ever. *"They saw me mess up. They'll think I'm slipping."*

Footsteps.

Jordan appears beside him, offering a water bottle.

Jordan: *"Dude. You crushed it. That was unreal."*

Mike shakes his head, staring at the floor.

Mike: *"No, I didn't. I messed up."*

Jordan frowns.

Jordan: *"Bro, seriously? No one even noticed. You didn't panic. You kept going. That's what matters."*

Mike wants to believe him. But the words don't quite sink in. The mistake still echoes.

But then—another thought breaks through.

"I finished. I didn't walk away. I didn't quit.". Something shifts.

Mike doesn't win first place.

But then— The judges announce a special recognition: "Best Resilience."

Mike freezes.

Murmurs ripple through the audience. *"Resilience? That's... new."*

His legs feel shaky as he stands. But something inside him feels steady. His name is called as the winder of the best resilience award.

As he walks onto the stage, the judge hands him the certificate with a knowing smile.

Judge: *"Mike your ability to stay composed under pressure today was remarkable. It's not about never making mistakes—it's about how you recover and learn from them."*

The audience applauds.

Mike takes a deep breath, looks out at the crowd.

The words land somewhere deep inside him. He grips the certificate tightly.

Mike: *"Thank you. That... really means a lot."* The weight on his shoulders feels lighter, finally after a long time.

Mike walks through the halls the next day.

People glance his way. But he doesn't feel like their stares define him.

Jordan catches up, grinning.

Jordan: *"See? Told you—you're tougher than you think."*

He holds up a fist.

Mike bumps it, smiling.

They walk in comfortable silence.

Mike exhales slowly, his mind clearing.

Mike: *"I guess I always thought being perfect was the only way to earn respect. But maybe... it's more about showing up, even when things don't go as planned."*

He glances around at his classmates, his shoulders relaxing just a little. *"I've been chasing the wrong goal. It's not about never messing up. It's about having the guts to keep going, even when it's tough."*

A small but powerful shift happens inside him.

The weight of perfection isn't completely gone, but it's lighter.

Mike still works hard, still gives his best, but it doesn't feel like his entire worth is on the line.

Mike now carries something more valuable than a first-place trophy.

Self-acceptance. Balance. A new perspective.

And unlike grades or awards, this is something no one can take from him.

It's a gift he's determined to hold onto, not just for himself... but for those around him. Because real strength isn't about never failing. It's about having the courage to keep going.

And now?

Mike knows he's strong enough.

Learning Lessons from "The Elixir"

You don't have to be perfect to be strong, respected, or worthy.

Mike's journey shows that real strength isn't about never making mistakes—it's about how you handle them. Everyone stumbles, but those moments of failure? That's where real courage is found.

It's okay to admit when things don't go as planned—it doesn't make you weak. It makes you human.

Mike didn't stop pushing himself—he just stopped tying his self-worth to being flawless. When he embraced his imperfections, he found more confidence, stronger friendships, and less pressure and more balance.

The same is true for you. Sharing your struggles doesn't make you weaker—it reminds others they're not alone.

To Bring with You

As you close this book, take a moment to reflect on the journeys you've just experienced. Each character, with their unique struggles and triumphs, has walked a path of growth—one that might feel familiar to your own. Whether they faced perfectionism, self-doubt, or the pressure to fit in, their stories share a common truth: strength is found not in chasing an ideal but in embracing who you are, imperfections and all.

The Lessons We've Learned

Through their adventures, these characters have shown us that life's challenges aren't roadblocks—they're stepping stones. Here are some truths you can carry with you:

- **Mistakes Are Part of the Journey:** Leo, Mauricio and the others have learned that setbacks don't define their worth. Whether it's a stumble in a debate or a struggle to fit in, every challenge is an opportunity to grow. When you face your own missteps, remember: they are simply lessons in disguise.
- **Self-Worth Comes from Within:** In a world that often measures success by achievements or appearance, it's easy to lose sight of what truly matters. But as these stories remind us, your value isn't tied to external validation. It comes from embracing your unique strengths and showing up as your authentic self.
- **Connection is a Source of Strength:** Throughout their journeys, the characters found support in unexpected places—a mentor's wisdom, a friend's encouragement, or even their own reflection. You don't have to face life's challenges alone. Trust in the people who see your potential, and don't be afraid to lean on them when you need it.

Your Own Hero's Journey

Every day, you're writing your own story. Like the characters in this book, you'll face trials that test your courage and resilience. Some days will be harder than others, but every step forward—no matter how small—counts.

- **Embrace Your Journey:** There's no single path to self-confidence or success. Your journey will be as unique as you are. Celebrate your progress, and give yourself grace on the days when it feels like you're standing still.
- **Define Success on Your Terms:** The world will always have expectations, but you have the power to decide what success means for you. Is it about grades? Friendships? Exploring your creativity? Whatever it is, let it be something that brings you joy and fulfillment.
- **Remember: You're Enough:** Not because of what you achieve, how you look, or how others perceive you. You're enough simply because you are.

A Final Thought

As you step back into your own life, know that every story—yours included—is a work in progress. There will be highs and lows, triumphs and setbacks. But with each experience, you're growing stronger, wiser, and more in tune with your true self.

Carry these stories with you as a reminder of your resilience, your worth, and your potential. When doubt creeps in, let the voices of these characters remind you: you're capable of far more than you think.

Now, it's your turn to be the hero of your own journey. Embrace the adventure, trust in your strength, and never forget—you are always enough.

The Next Chapter Awaits

The book may end here, but your story continues. Take what you've learned, apply it in your own life, and know that you have everything you need to thrive. Go forward with courage, confidence, and the knowledge that your journey is yours to shape.

To bring with you wherever you go in life: hope, courage, and the unwavering belief in your own potential.

About the Authors

At Aria Capri Publishing, we are dedicated to fostering fun and growth through learning for children and teens. Our mission is to empower young minds to explore their unique journeys, embrace their potential, and trust in their ability to grow. With an open mind and a spirit of curiosity, every child and teen can take steps toward a brighter future.

We know young people are natural learners—eager and ready to absorb knowledge in their own way. Recognizing that there's no one-size-fits-all approach to personal growth, we create interactive books rooted in science-backed research. Our goal is to nurture developing minds while inspiring confidence, resilience, and a lifelong love of learning.

As parents ourselves, we understand your desire to see your children and teens thrive. That's why our books are designed to support readers of all ages in building a growth mindset and realizing their unique potential.

We're Mauricio and Devon, a husband-and-wife team with a shared passion for lifelong learning and personal growth. After the birth of our son, Leonardo, we were inspired to create something meaningful—not just for her but for families everywhere. Leonardo is our motivation. Together, we're committed to helping children and teens grow into their brightest, most confident selves.

Thank You for Reading!

We hope this book has inspired confidence and growth for the teen girl in your life. If you found value in these stories, we'd love to hear your thoughts! Your review can help others discover this book and make a difference in the lives of more young readers.

To leave a review, simply scan the QR code below or visit the platform where you purchased this book. Your support as a reader means everything and helps us continue creating empowering content.

Thank you for being part of this journey!

Warm regards,

Devon & Mauricio